T0285775

"Archie Jones breaks down *how* to define, assess, and improve your leadership capital aka "the currency of change". His coaching superpower comes through the conversational read peppered with examples and questions for your reflection. *The Treasure You Seek* offers a framework for closing the leadership gap on the road to unlocking your full potential."

Laetitia Tiani Vessah
Principal, Leo Legacy; Harvard Business School Alumni/Former Student of Archie Jones

"Good leaders provide direction, purpose, and reason for a group or organization to follow. They also share their knowledge, wisdom, and experience with others. Their leadership becomes a calling to serve others. Archie is a leader who has risen to his position through his actions and his words. His thoughts on leadership and influence are clear, specific, and on target in today's business and social climate."

David A. Thomas, PhD
President, Morehouse College

"Archie has the rare ability to make anyone look deeper at themselves and see new possibilities for their lives. His leadership capital framework can apply to people and leaders from all walks of life, even those who may have never recognized that they are a leader themselves. If you don't know what your superpower is yet, this book will help you discover it."

Everette Taylor
CEO, Kickstarter

"There is no greater aha moment than figuring out your superpower. *The Treasure You Seek* is an inspiring book that clearly lays out a powerful roadmap to finding one's superpower. This book is a must-read for anyone seeking to become a more effective and more fulfilled leader."

Vanessa Kirsch
Founder-in-Residence and Senior Partner, New Profit Inc.

"As I read Archie's book, all bells started to go off in my head! His early career leadership lessons are very impactful and resonate very much with me. At 32 years old I was one of the youngest CFOs of a NYSE listed company with a team of about 1,000 people under my responsibility. My early approach to leadership was purely transactional. I thought my job was just about getting my team to perform certain tasks that I directed them to do. I even made the mistake of trying to perform 'management by email.' I was *so* wrong! I wish I had Archie's book early in my career and had then learned his concept of 'leadership capital.' I would have been much more effective and impactful! And it would have saved me many mistakes."

Alvaro Rodriguez-Arregui
Cofounder, IGNIA; Former Chairman of the Board, ACCION

"In *The Treasure You Seek,* Archie Jones navigates readers through his remarkable personal story and provides an essential, heartfelt, and strategic guide to leadership in today's business climate. Archie powerfully illustrates the importance of harnessing community to both shape and achieve the "treasure" at the heart of a successful business world journey. *The Treasure You Seek* provides an emerging generation of previously underinvested business leaders concrete guidance on how to develop and own their trajectories and, ultimately, their success."

Clara Wu Tsai
Owner, Brooklyn Nets; Founder, Joe and Clara Tsai Foundation

"I've known Archie since we were classmates at Harvard Business School. However, notwithstanding our relationship as peers, as I read *The Treasure You Seek*, I wished I too could have benefitted from his office hours! As Archie says, that's why he wrote this inspiring and uplifting book—to make his office hours experience available to as wide an audience as possible. Archie's 5 Cs Leadership Capital framework captures succinctly and powerfully outlines the key elements that underpin professional and personal success! Leaders of all ages and experience levels can benefit from this book."

Victor Williams
CEO, NBA Africa

the

Treasure
You Seek

A Guide to
Developing and Leveraging
Your Leadership Capital

Archie L. Jones, Jr.

Forbes | Books

Published by Forbes Books, Charleston, South Carolina.
An imprint of Advantage Media Group.

Forbes Books is a registered trademark, and the Forbes Books colophon is a trademark of Forbes Media, LLC.

Printed in the United States of America.

10 9 8 7 6 5 4 3 2 1

ISBN: 979-8-88750-215-1 (Hardcover)
ISBN: 979-8-88750-216-8 (eBook)

Library of Congress Control Number: 2023919421

Book design by Wesley Strickland.

This custom publication is intended to provide accurate information and the opinions of the author in regard to the subject matter covered. It is sold with the understanding that the publisher, Forbes Books, is not engaged in rendering legal, financial, or professional services of any kind. If legal advice or other expert assistance is required, the reader is advised to seek the services of a competent professional.

Since 1917, Forbes has remained steadfast in its mission to serve as the defining voice of entrepreneurial capitalism. Forbes Books, launched in 2016 through a partnership with Advantage Media, furthers that aim by helping business and thought leaders bring their stories, passion, and knowledge to the forefront in custom books. Opinions expressed by Forbes Books authors are their own. To be considered for publication, please visit **books.Forbes.com**.

To my mom, Lillian Jones, for being a role model of cultivating humanity through education. To my dad, Archie Jones, Sr., for being a role model of creating opportunity through entrepreneurship. Thank you both for your love and support in my pursuit of my treasure.

Contents

Introduction

Teaching is more than imparting knowledge; it is inspiring change. Learning is more than absorbing facts; it is acquiring understanding.

—*WILLIAM ARTHUR WARD*

Around the time I started writing this book, I took a group of students from my entrepreneurship class at Harvard Business School (HBS) out for coffee and a discussion of how they were applying the lessons of the class to their own lives. I do this pretty regularly, and even though it's informal, I've realized that a lot of my most powerful teaching moments come out of this type of setting, whether it's at a coffee shop or a one-on-one conversation in my office hours. In the classroom, I may be up in front of eighty or ninety people, delivering the same curriculum to each of them. That's sort of my opening salvo. But one-on-one or in a small group, we can start to have different conversations.

In this particular case, one of the students who joined me for coffee was a young woman who was taking time away from her job with one of the big consulting firms to come to HBS for a couple of years and obtain her MBA. As I went around the group asking where each student was on their entrepreneurial journey, I could tell that this woman felt unsure of where she was headed. When it was her turn to speak, she told us that she was worried that simply returning to her consulting job after business school was just the path of least resistance. What she really felt called to do was be a social entrepreneur, even though she hadn't quite figured out what that would look like yet.

As we talked through the possibilities, she realized that there were social enterprise opportunities within her consulting firm, where she would be going back to work for the summer between her first and second years at HBS. From my perspective, the stakes are generally fairly low for this kind of in-between summer work, although the students certainly don't see it this way. Still, I encourage them to take some risks, step out of their comfort zone, and try to do something during the summer to move themselves toward what they really want to do after they finish business school—whether that's as large as a 180-degree career shift or as small as exploring work in a new geographic area.

During the course of the meeting, this young woman realized that she was valuable enough to her employer to negotiate for some more flexibility in the type of projects she worked on, and she resolved to request for her employer to place her in a position on one of the firm's social enterprise projects. She left the meeting with the confidence to communicate what she wanted and thanked me for talking it through with her.

With conversations like this that I have with students over coffee and in office hours, I get to communicate the deeper, more personal type of message that you'll find in this book. Personal to me, because it gives me the opportunity to share my own leadership journey and the challenges I've faced on my path from private equity to teaching at HBS. But also personal to the individual I'm speaking to, helping them leverage their leadership capital (which I explain in chapter 1) to make progress on their own path to the treasure they seek—whatever that treasure is and however they define it.

Through HBS and other teaching and coaching settings where I get to speak directly to audiences, I'm able to communicate with maybe a few hundred people a year. And even with the diverse and global student body at HBS, those whom I can coach individually are still only a small subset of the people around the world who could benefit, and who deserve to benefit, from the lessons I teach. That's why I wrote this book. It's the best way to simulate that one-on-one conversation—where the magic really happens—with a much broader audience.

HBS states as its mission, "We educate leaders who make a difference in the world." I know that there are a lot of leaders out there hoping to make a difference who will never have access to HBS. This book is my attempt to do my part to inspire and prepare those people as well.

So, welcome to my office hours.

Coaching, from Wall Street to the Classroom

I've been coaching all my life—even before I thought about it that way. When I started my career, I didn't think of myself as a coach. I had majored in accounting at Morehouse, but late in my college career, I got excited about finance. I was particularly intrigued by the world of private equity and ultimately decided I wanted to get into that game. I knew you could make a good living there, but more importantly, I was fascinated by the beauty of this idea of creating value in an organization through strategy and hard work so that you could end up with an organization valued at two to three times its original valuation. After college I ended up in an internship on Wall Street that ultimately led to a job doing what I wanted to do.

At age twenty-seven, after my MBA, I was working at a consulting group called Parthenon as a junior private equity associate under a VP named Samantha. Hoping to take on more responsibility and eventually lead my own transaction, I started doing more of *her* job—drafting agreements, reviewing legal documents, and so forth. I didn't care if I got credit or whether it was in my job description. I was just hungry to build my skills and wanted to take the lead on transactions of buying and selling companies. Samantha didn't mind, and in fact, she encouraged it—it took work off her plate so that she could do *her* boss's job.

After a year or so of this arrangement, a potential deal came to the firm that none of the first-chair VPs had the bandwidth for. By this time, Samantha was able to vouch for me that I was able to do first-chair work, so I was able to step into the position of point person on that transaction even though it was above my pay grade and title. It looked like it would be a smaller deal, and there were no big-name brands involved, so our managing partners just said, "Sure, let Archie work on that."

I even took the initial call alone, talking with the company leaders who were thinking about who they wanted to partner with, about why they should partner with us. After all the usual questions about the fundamentals of the deal, I simply asked, "What are you looking for in a partner?" The COO of the company, Troy, who is now a good buddy of mine, tells me that they had never been asked that question before. That opened up a constructive line of communication and won what ended up being a very lucrative deal for my firm.

The main person I was partnering with on the deal was the founder and owner, Rudy Karsan. Rudy, more than a decade my senior, had never raised outside capital from a private equity group, so he was still fairly new to the process that I had been practicing and studying up on my whole career. That meant that I played the role of more than just the finance guy. I walked Rudy through how to think about the transaction: what does he want out of it, does he really want to go through with it, and what will the outcome look like? Fortunately, Rudy is brilliant and a fast learner; as an actuary, he has developed the ability to quickly absorb data and information and apply it to his advantage.

For the entire three months we were doing due diligence on the transaction, Rudy and I were on the phone constantly, discussing everything from the specifics of the deal to broader business strategy. Through it all, though I didn't think of it this way at the time, I was *coaching* Rudy on all things to do with this transaction. Those Saturday evening phone calls were the beginning of my office hour sessions.

The whole time I was a little worried that Rudy was going to ask how old I was. Junior associates didn't usually take on deals like this, and I did my best throughout the process to project an older, much more experienced presence—not the presence of a guy doing his very first deal. He eventually did bring it up just as the deal was closing, and when I told him, he said, "Wow, I thought at least we'd be of the same generation!" Still, when it came to selecting two new members for his board of directors, he tapped me alongside a senior partner because he knew he could rely on me to act as his coach and to share my experience to make his team better.

That first board position laid the groundwork for a lot of the success I had in the area of private equity, and it all came from coaching. I also became the go-to guy inside my own firm for my peers and other junior associates who wanted to know how I'd pulled off this transaction. So I started coaching internally to the firm as well.

It wasn't until years later, though, that I realized (through an experience I'll describe in chapter 2) that coaching and teaching were my superpowers. When I found that out, I embarked on the next phase of my leadership journey, which would lead me to being a coach in several contexts, including teaching at HBS, and including writing this book.

Leadership Capital and the 5 Cs

You may think a leadership book is not for you. You may not be a corporate titan, a politician, a community leader, or someone's boss. The good news is that you don't have to be any of these things to be a leader. If you have a goal, a treasure you're seeking, and you can enlist the help of others to achieve that goal, then you are at least potentially a leader, and you can benefit from learning how to leverage your leadership capital in the way I describe in this book. Leadership is not about title or status but about influence and impact.

Leadership capital, as I explain in chapter 1, consists in the resources you have that can empower you to work with others to achieve your goal. The 5 Cs that I outline in the rest of the chapters are tools to develop and leverage that leadership capital:

1. Capability

2. Culture

3. Communication

4. Connection

5. Confidence

I'll describe each of these in depth, telling both my own and others' stories of how they helped us on our leadership journeys.

The leadership capital framework and the 5 Cs came about as a result of my reflecting on how I've achieved the success that I have had. They formalize the basic principles that helped me on my leadership journey and got me to where I am today. I didn't necessarily think of them as "5 Cs" when I was on that journey, but after becoming a professor at HBS, I started getting requests to share my story to provide guidance and coaching for young people through organizations like Year Up (which I'll talk more about later). For easy reference, I started placing the insights and lessons I had learned into a framework for presentation. That framework developed into the leadership capital framework, along with the 5 Cs. They were my way of packaging my own journey to present to an audience as the keys to my success.

Now, I know that the leadership capital framework resonates across cultures for a broad array of different people. I've taught the 5 Cs around the world, and even in my class right now, I'm talking to more than eighty students from twenty-four countries every week. I'm giving the same message, but it finds application and resonates across continents—so I'm confident that, whatever treasure you seek and wherever you are on your leadership journey, it will resonate for you too.

I spent most of my career focusing on investing financial capital. I've invested hundreds of millions of dollars, generated great returns, and helped create value for myself and others. But I don't think that's where I can be most helpful moving forward. I'm more interested now in helping people invest their *leadership* capital to create value for themselves and to attain success however they define it. It doesn't have to be monetary (although it might be). The treasure you seek may be social impact, political influence, productive community engagement, or creating and leading a healthy, happy family. *Whatever* treasure you seek, leadership capital is the resource to help you get there.

Similarly, leadership capital is what leaders will use to change their world—no matter how big or small that world is. It could be the private world of their own family, their own community, or something much larger scale. This will be specific to you—to what success means to you and where you are on your leadership journey. In any case, the leadership capital framework will provide the ingredients to help you develop the influence to make the kind of change you want to see in your world.

CHAPTER 1:

Leadership Capital

Leadership is not domination, but the art of persuading people to work toward a common goal.

—DANIEL GOLEMAN

My leadership journey started probably before I even knew what leadership was. I certainly hadn't started thinking about leadership capital or about myself as a leader. I was just an eleven-year-old playing peewee football.

I had been playing for a few years, as a wide receiver on offense and as a defensive back, but this particular year, the coach pulled me aside during the preseason and told me he wanted me to play quarterback (QB).

I looked around at the other players. We were still getting to know one another and figuring out who was who, but I knew other kids had played QB before, so they had to have more experience and physical capability. My best friend, a pitcher in baseball, was also on the team, so I knew I didn't have the best arm. I did not feel either qualified or ready. I was thinking, *You want me to do what now?* But

I said exactly what my upbringing as a polite Southern young man dictated: "Yes, sir, I'll try."

As the season got underway, I expected the coach to realize his mistake, pull me out of the QB position, and put one of those other kids in. But that isn't what happened. We ended up having a tremendous season, were nearly undefeated, and won the local peewee football championship.

Our success throughout that season had me thinking differently about what I was capable of. I don't know exactly what the coach saw in me that made him put me at QB, but he saw some kind of leadership potential, and that leadership potential developed over the course of the season.

The QB is the coach on the field, both in the huddle and on the offensive line—leading the huddle, helping call plays, and driving ten other people (in this case, kids) toward that goal line. I had to be able to tell a story and say the right things to get those kids to do what they might not otherwise want to do.

One game, deep in the season, one of my offensive linemen was outweighed by his defender by what must have been 50 pounds. I couldn't get a single play off, because this big kid just crashed through the line every single time. My linemen were scared of getting flattened, and the rest of the team was getting discouraged thinking we were going to lose the game. I told all of them, "Look, I just need you to buy me three seconds. I know you're tired and frustrated, but all I need is three seconds to get a pass off. Three seconds, and we'll be good."

They did it. And they managed to keep doing it, play after play, and we were able to start moving the ball again. I had been able to tell them a new story of how we were going to win, three seconds at a time, and it got everyone focused, back in the game, and oriented toward our goal, which we were eventually able to attain. As I'll discuss later in this book, we shifted from a big-picture focus to a focus on small wins, which allowed us to make a little progress at a time, build our confidence, and ultimately achieve the larger goal—not a bad recipe for when you're feeling stuck and want to start making some progress!

Coach Wycoff gave me the opportunity to start to develop leadership in myself. During the season I developed a belief in myself that I could carry forward with me. From there it was up to me to start making my own opportunities, from traveling abroad as an ambassador for my high school and my hometown, to becoming president of my class at Morehouse, and finally to Wall Street. The same lessons applied in every case, but first I had to believe I could be successful.

It's easy to talk ourselves out of this belief. I was lucky that I was conditioned to say "Yes, sir" to a coach, because my impulse in the moment he told me he wanted me at QB was to say, "I'm not the right person." We tell ourselves versions of this all the time: *I'm not the right person for the job. The timing isn't right.* Any excuse to stay in our comfort zone.

In this book I've packaged up the lessons I've learned and made use of over the last forty years to offer to others, to give you the opportunity to find the leader hidden within yourself. It's what I love about coaching. I've seen the power that someone offering that opportunity can have. So I'm here to do for you what Coach Wycoff did for me: create opportunity and educate, inspire, and empower you to make the most of that opportunity.

What Is Leadership?

My aim in this book is to help you, the reader—no matter who you are—establish and build your leadership capital. It doesn't matter if you don't see yourself as a leader. You don't have to be anyone's boss, a corporate leader, or a politician. All it takes to begin your leadership journey is a goal—a treasure you are seeking.

Leadership has nothing to do with title, status, or seniority. Leadership is distinct from management, although good managers can certainly benefit from leveraging their leadership capital. Leadership is not about being anyone's "boss."

Leadership, as I describe it in this book, is *a process of social influence that maximizes the efforts of others toward the achievement of a goal*.[1] If you have a goal (whether it's your personal goal or a goal internal to some organization that you're a part of) and you have other people whom you're in social relationships with, then *you are a leader*, at least potentially.

Confusing leadership with title, status, or being a boss actually makes for bad leaders. You end up focusing more on being served by others than serving the others in order to maximize their influence and get them on your team. Just like me with the peewee football team, a leader and those they lead have a *shared destiny*.

Many of history's greatest leaders, the ones whose legacy echoes across generations, started out with a deficit in the status and title department. Their legacy stands in what they did for other people and for the sake of a larger goal. A personal hero who inspires me and who I often think back to is Harriet Tubman, who started her own leadership journey as an escape to freedom out of enslavement. Tubman's example, which I return to elsewhere in this book, is an extreme one, but it goes to show that even the greatest of leaders have to start from where they are, whatever the disadvantages and lack of resources that entails.

The Currency of Change

So we've rethought leadership; now, what is leadership *capital*?

Capital, in any area, is a measure of the resources a person has to make an impact. It operates like a currency, and of course, the most

---

1   Kevin Kruse, *What is Leadership?* Forbes, April 9, 2013. https://www.forbes.com/sites/kevinkruse/2013/04/09/what-is-leadership/?sh=157908c15b90

natural analogy is money. At Harvard Business School (HBS), I teach a course on scaling minority businesses, and much of the conversation is about *accessing and leveraging capital.* Now, of course, since it's a simple analogy, and since scaling a business does require money, students (and people in general) tend to think of the capital that needs to get leveraged entirely in terms of *financial* capital.

Don't get me wrong—financial capital is very important to a business. But it needs to work in concert with other forms of capital. Students (and entrepreneurs) fall into the trap of thinking that if they can just get the money they need, they can get done what they want to get done. However, if I give you money to seed your business, but you don't really know what you're doing because you've never done it before, your odds of success go way down. So you also need *experience capital.* Likewise, if you don't have a network or know any of the right people to help you scale your business, you're going to struggle mightily. You need social capital or, as I call it, *relationship capital.*

Forms of Capital

All of these forms of capital function to enable you to create and capture the value of opportunities. Just as having cash on hand allows you to buy stuff, having know-how and a network (experience capital and relationship capital) empowers you to take advantage of an opportunity when it presents itself—or, better yet, allows you to create opportunities for yourself and others. In each case, the more of something you want, whether that's a good or service or the attainment of a goal, the more capital you're going to need to get you there. Change, growth, and impact all require capital.

How does leadership capital fit in? Your ability to build and leverage the other forms of capital is built on leadership capital, which is *the measure of the resources you have to drive the process of influencing others to achieve your goal.* Leadership capital is foundational to the value of the other forms of capital—you need it to be able to attract and leverage the others and to maximize the value you get from them. In the chapters that follow, we talk about experience capital in terms of capability and culture and relationship capital in terms of communication and connection. Developing these will all be part of the leadership capital journey.

Leadership capital is the currency of change. It's what you need in order to be able to drive whatever level of change you hope to achieve. The more change you want to deliver, the more leadership capital that change requires. Attaining your goals, whatever they are, will require some experience and relationship capital, as well as some financial capital, even if it's just to keep putting food on the table while you go after your other goals. If you're looking to attract, manage, and develop those forms of capital, the leadership capital framework is your path to getting there.

The 5 Cs of Leadership Capital

The core of the leadership capital framework is the 5 Cs:

Each one of these is a tool or building block for developing and deploying leadership capital. In the chapters that follow, I walk you through these one by one. I tell my own story of locating and learning to implement each component, and I will share the stories of others doing the same thing so that you can see different ways to apply each C to your own situation. Each of the 5 Cs plays some role in every leadership journey—even in my season as QB of my peewee football team.

CAPABILITY

The first two Cs are all about self-knowledge and introspection, and the first one, *capability*, is about *knowing your superpower*. To discover your superpower, your unique capability, you need to dig deep into both the skills you've acquired over your lifetime and the unique talents that you were born with or that seem to come naturally to you. Whatever that superpower is, that is the cornerstone of how you contribute, whether that's in your contribution to the larger goal of some organization or in what you bring to the accomplishment of your own goals. Your capability journey lies in the uncovering of your superpower combined with the continual building of your other knowledge and skill sets.

Like I said, I'm still not sure what capability my coach saw in eleven-year-old me, but he saw something that made him put me in the QB position. I had some know-how (experience capital) playing on both sides of the ball as a receiver and as a defensive back, and maybe he saw some innate coaching potential (*my* superpower) in the way I interacted with the other kids. Whatever the case may be, that capability, especially that coaching and encouraging potential, was the groundwork for the success I was able to help create that season.

CULTURE

Figuring out the culture component again requires some self-examination, to determine what specific values and what unique lens on the world you bring to situations in order to leverage your unique voice and perspective in the pursuit of your goals or your organization's goals. Understanding your culture will allow you to bring your whole self and the value that you have to offer to your journey, whether that's in work, with family, or in the community.

In peewee football, even eleven-year-olds come to the team with their own ingrained ideas about how the game should be played and what roles everyone ought to play. (With eleven-year-olds in particular, everyone thinks they should be the one to run the ball and score touchdowns!) Each one of those perspectives has to be understood to help them fuse together into a positive, team-wide approach. My best buddy, who I mentioned had a stronger arm than me, ended up playing center with me as QB. Our being best friends was a cultural ingredient in how well we were able to work together that season.

COMMUNICATION

With communication, we move into the world of tools for leveraging your relationship capital in order to influence others to achieve goals. On your leadership capital journey, you want to communicate two primary things. First, you need to tell the world what your superpower is—be honest about the unique value you offer. Second, you need to tell the world where you want to go on your leadership journey—be up front about the treasure you seek. There is wisdom in the saying *Ask, and you shall receive*. Often, we aren't able to get what we want simply because we're afraid to communicate our desires to others. Effective communication positions you for opportunities to pursue your own treasure, to join other people's journeys, and to bring others along on your journey with you as well.

One of the principles of communication, as I like to put it, is *Ask for the order*. This is what I did when I pulled a scared and frustrated team together in a huddle and said, "Look guys, I just need you to get me three seconds." Asking for the order has enormous power.

CONNECTION

With connection, we put our communication skills to work helping others on their journeys and getting help from them on our journey, in turn—investing in others and getting them to invest in us. If you're seeking your treasure, you're not going to be able to get to it alone, which brings us to another basic principle of the leadership capital framework: *The answer is in your network*. Reaching out and leveraging that network enables you to lighten your own load on your journey and cover more ground more quickly or with less effort.

I built connections with other kids on my football team based on what they needed in order to be on board—some of them I knew

I had to be tough with, while others needed a softer approach. And I knew I needed them. The QB can't do it alone; he needs every one of those ten other people to be in it with him. That's part of the magic of team sports: it teaches kids from a very young age that it doesn't matter how good *you* are (or how good you think you are). What matters is getting others to get on board with you and helping them realize that you're all in the journey together.

CONFIDENCE

Confidence is not about being unafraid. It's about not letting fear, especially fear of failure, prevent your forward progress. This is the true definition of courage. The last principle of the leadership capital framework comes from the work of Joseph Campbell and is the source of this book's title: *The cave you are afraid to enter holds the treasure you seek.* At some point on your quest for that treasure, you will have to enter that cave. This also involves some introspection, because figuring out what your cave is—what you fear the most in your journey—will also tell you where you need to go looking for your treasure. Confidence consists of tools and strategies for mustering the courage to enter these unknown and uncomfortable stages of your journey.

I did not feel qualified or prepared to take on the position of QB at eleven years old, but I stepped into it, and I built the skills during the course of the season to bolster the confidence in myself and my teammates to forge ahead even when we faced challenges. This often meant starting with small wins—just *this* first down, which will lead us to *this* touchdown, and then the progress starts to build on itself. More than anything, the confidence I developed that season to handle myself when getting thrown into something new and unknown is what I carried with me into other spheres and to my future successes. I knew that, at least in some cases, I could deliver on something I had never done before if someone asked me to, and I had the confidence to dive in.

* * *

This book walks you through the 5 Cs in order to help you develop and deploy your leadership capital step-by-step. With each one, you can start from exactly where you are and focus on making progress in one area at a time, just a little bit at a time, in order to build yourself up toward attaining your treasure. If we just look straight at the goal, and at the distance between where we are now and where that treasure is, the gap can be overwhelming and paralyzing. It's important to know and reflect on what treasure you're seeking, but that doesn't mean that's where all of your focus should be. The work of leadership capital and the 5 Cs, which is designed to take you far along that quest, takes place here in the day-to-day of putting one building block on top of another. This investment in yourself will start to show some early returns as you go along, and your leadership capital will begin to grow as other people begin to see that you're worth *their* investment. As you build leadership capital, the other forms of capital will also begin to come your way as others start to invest more and more in you. But you have to make that initial investment.

The Leadership Journey

The shape of your own personal leadership journey depends on what your goals are—what treasure you seek. Whether your goals only pertain to you and your family or close inner circle, or you hope to be the kind of leader of movements who changes the world, you have to start where you are, and you have to start with yourself. I like to think of a person and their social relationships as a set of concentric rings. The inner ring is just yourself, and that's where you have to start. That's why the first couple of Cs focus so much on introspection and self-examination.

Leadership and Impact Journey

(Follows the Harriet Tubman Journey)

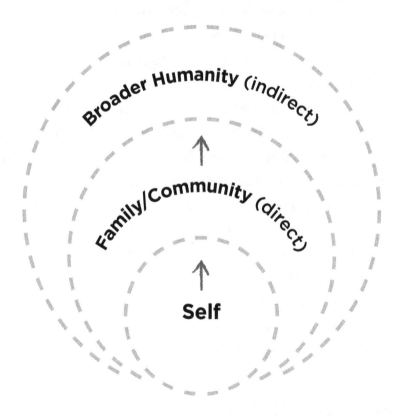

The Journey

1. **Self gets stronger** (capability, culture, and confidence)
2. **Invest in your community and broader humanity** (communication, connection, and confidence)

    *Outer two rings grow faster than self

Harriet Tubman's leadership journey, which was also a journey from enslavement to freedom both for herself and others, follows the path through these concentric rings. Her first priority was to get herself free. She managed her own escape and then came back for her family. That's her second ring. Your second ring is your family and immediate community—people you know directly. Once you've taken advantage of opportunities at that innermost ring—whether that's your own introspection or Tubman getting herself free—you're able to start aiming for change at the level of your second ring, like Tubman getting her family out of enslavement.

The third ring out is the wider world—all those people whom you don't have direct contact with. Once you've developed your leadership and are taking advantage of opportunities in your second ring, you can start to leverage that leadership capital to create larger, third-ring opportunities. This is the realm of broader social impact and significance, which is where many people's treasure lies. That's one of the ways I'm trying to make change with this book. For Tubman, her third-ring work lay in her organizing work with the Underground Railroad and her activism in working toward the abolition of slavery overall. Third-ring leadership is what cements a leader's legacy. Harriet Tubman personally walked to freedom with dozens of people, but her activism touched millions.

That said, some people may not have goals that reach significantly out to their third ring. Their goals touch their second ring—their neighborhood, their church, their family. The treasure they seek is a local one. This is no less valuable, and they are no less a leader. The lessons in the development of leadership capital I offer here will benefit that person, too. Even if you're still working on yourself, if the treasure you're seeking right now is a purely personal one, it requires some level of leadership—not just self-leadership but also leveraging a network of support. And you have to get yourself to a stable place in order to start leveraging leadership capital at the second and third rings.

Your rings can shrink and grow, too. Part of growing your leadership capital and building your network will involve bringing people from your third ring into your second ring. This is the work of communication and connection—reaching out to people and building an enlarging network.

Your relationship to opportunity also shapes your leadership journey. You may start at a more passive level, taking the opportunities that are presented to you. Even then, you may benefit from coaching in learning to recognize opportunities when they appear and developing the confidence to act on them. You will have advanced in your leadership journey, however, when you start creating the opportunities for yourself. This requires a bit more leadership capital, as it most likely means reaching out to and leveraging your network, or creating that network if you haven't yet. Creating opportunity requires you to reach outside of yourself a little bit more.

These concepts are all interrelated. The more opportunity you want to create and the wider out into your second or third ring you want to have impact, the more leadership capital you need. As you start effectively investing leadership capital at the first- and second-ring levels, you start to get a return on that capital—more people start investing their capital in you. From there, you can start to invest it more broadly, in more people, across a wider network.

Learning from Others

I'm going to take you through my own leadership journey, covering some important personal milestones: becoming a high-performing private equity professional, getting on an S&P 500 board of directors, teaching at one of the best business schools in the world, and working with some of the most effective impact investing groups. The lessons here are what got me where I am, to the treasure I seek. I have also helped others, such as some game-changing leaders in impact investing, to leverage the same lessons in order to achieve great significance in their own spheres.

In other words, I've pulled some folks from my third ring into my second ring. For example, *Terri Bradley* is an Atlanta-based entrepreneur whose company, Brown Toy Box, produces educational games and toys that represent characters of color so that children of color (and their parents) will see themselves represented when they play and learn. They also work to interrupt generational cycles of poverty by using educational toys to introduce ideas in science, tech, engineering, the arts, and math (STEAM) to help prepare kids for the careers of the future. Terri started her business as a single mom driven by a passion for helping kids and has grown the company to the point where it was named one of Oprah's Favorite Things in 2022. I'm an adviser to Terri and an advisory board member for the company.

I connected with Greg Walton through the network around Year Up, where he had been an intern about fifteen years ago. Year Up provides tuition-free job training for young adults with low-to-moderate income and no college degree. The young people who go into Year Up are smart and hardworking but haven't been able to meet their full potential, typically because of life circumstances and lack of opportunities. Year Up provides these young people the opportunity to change that trajectory and to substantially grow and leverage their experience and relationship capital.

I've worked with Year Up for several years, serving on their national board, mentoring several students, and speaking to groups of students. Greg is a major Year Up success story, having gone into the program after a short period of being incarcerated and working his way to a senior executive position in the IT division at the Massachusetts Institute of Technology (MIT). He's now vice chair of the national board for Year Up as well, and I'm coaching and advising him in his goal to get on the board of a public company and start to leverage his leadership capital in new ways.

Terri and Greg both started out at a socioeconomic disadvantage, and both can tell you a leadership journey story that includes all of the 5 Cs. We'll hear from them in later chapters, to illustrate some of the ways in which the leadership journey takes a similar shape even for different people who are seeking different types of treasure.[2] I'm also going to tell a story that exemplifies many of my HBS students through the example of Benedita.[3] Her journey, which we'll follow through her two years of business school, provides still another illustration of how anyone can deploy the leadership capital framework and the 5 Cs in their own quest.

Benedita, who is pursuing her MBA and is unsure of what she wants to do after she finishes, started her leadership journey as a consultant at the firm BCG. She will make good money going back to being a generalist consultant at BCG, but, like the woman I described in the introduction, she worries that this is the path of least resistance. What she really wants is to have a social impact back in her hometown of São Paulo, Brazil. Like Terri and Greg, Benedita is someone from humble beginnings who ends up creating opportunities for herself to chase her dream and have an impact on her broader community.

---

2   Quotes from Terri Bradley and Greg Walton are from interviews conducted with them on June 15, 2023, and June 12, 2023, respectively. Quotes have only been lightly edited for clarity and flow.

3   Benedita is not a real student—because of the Family Educational Rights and Privacy Act (FERPA), I would not be able to disclose this kind of specific information about a student, so she is fictional. She is also, however, a true-to-life amalgam of the hundreds of students I've worked with whose journeys exemplify the leadership capital framework and the 5 Cs.

We'll track her journey through all of the 5 Cs, beginning and ending with *confidence*—I first start having conversations with her because she fears she is not going to do well in my introduction to finance class. By the end of her journey (and the book), you will see her building the confidence to create and capture the opportunity to pursue her own treasure.

My first conversation with Benedita was in my office hours (if you read the introduction, you'll know how important those are). Though she had been an engineering major and was strong on the technical side of math, she was intimidated by the world of finance, which involved unfamiliar concepts and approaches. She hadn't had the opportunity to build a strong foundation in the basics of investing and financial capital, which she would need for her MBA. As I talked to her, I realized that she was due to learn one of the fundamental messages of this book: that the cave you fear to enter contains the treasure you seek. She could take the comfortable route and go back to being a tactical ops consultant at BCG—it certainly suited her technically oriented mind. But if she wanted to pursue her passion (her love for her hometown) and her dream (social impact), she was going to have to enter the cave, which in her case was the world of finance and investments.

It took a few meetings for Benedita to open up to me about what her dream and her passion were. Students like to start out by playing it close to the vest and are often afraid to communicate what they really want deep down; like most students, Benedita came to me because she was concerned about a grade. But that concern opens up onto a whole other conversation.

Benedita's story shows that the lessons of this book are already out in the world, being used by others and resonating with people. This book is my way of getting them out to a larger audience than the people I can have direct contact with. Just as the lessons have seeded the attainment of treasure for others, I hope that they can seed whatever your dreams are as well.

I want to help people create opportunities and leverage their leadership capital to take advantage of those opportunities. That's my goal as a coach. I even have an acronym for COACH: *create opportunity and cultivate humanity*. (Yes, the trademark has been filed on that, by the way.) I want you investing in yourself in pursuit of the treasure you seek, and I want others to see you as worth investing their own leadership capital in as well. And it doesn't stop there. Ultimately, what we can achieve together is a community of people coinvesting their leadership capital in one another to accomplish huge goals and effect enormous change. We just have to start where you are.

Prompts for Reflection

- Reflect on your leadership journey thus far. Where are you on your journey, and what progress have you already made?

- Where do you want to be in your journey? How broadly in your second or even third ring do you want to have impact? What treasure do you seek?

- The gap between where you are and where you want to be is the place where you need to do the work of going through the 5 Cs.

- Take an inventory of your assets in the areas of experience capital and relationship capital, just as you might do a budget of your finances. How much of these do you have, and how much will you need to attain your treasure? Where is the shortfall?

- Working on the fundamental areas of leadership capital—the 5 Cs—will help you make up that shortfall.

- If you want to dig deeper, visit www.archieljonesjr.com/assessment to take a leadership capital self-assessment in which you can score yourself on the components of the framework. You can then refer to the chapters in the book to help you in areas where you score low.

CHAPTER 2:

Capability: My Story

To know yourself is the beginning of wisdom.

—SOCRATES

My superpower journey began when I started feeling unsatisfied. I was about twenty years into my career and had taken on a position as CFO at a start-up. I had attained the title I wanted, the big goal for a finance professional. I was leveraging my finance skills, but I found that I wasn't thrilled to be exercising those muscles. It felt like something was missing. I was doing a limited amount of coaching work internally to the company (though I didn't see it as coaching at the time), but I wasn't having the kind of broader impact I wanted to have. I just wasn't enjoying it. *If I were doing what I'm supposed to do,* I thought, *it wouldn't feel this hard.*

I was working in Atlanta and not traveling as much as I had in the days when I was in private equity and building my network. During those years, I had just ticked steadily and comfortably along without really thinking about what my superpower was. All my experience and credentials up to that time were pointing me toward where it seemed I

29

ought to be as a finance professional: a CFO. I had achieved the title, and I got to travel less and spend more time at home. I had all the external markers of having arrived at my destination—but it didn't feel like I'd attained my treasure. Why did I feel like I was missing out? I was good at what I did, but I didn't feel *great* at what I did. And I wasn't excited.

So that was the bad news. The good news is that, like a lot of people, in a time of dissatisfaction, I had the opportunity to do some self-assessment and to look for strength in places I hadn't looked before.

Less travel meant that I had more time and opportunity to set down some professional roots for myself in Atlanta. I started exploring and ended up deciding to participate in a leadership development program offered by Leadership Atlanta. Every year they offer a nine-month program for leaders in the community to connect with one another and work on their leadership together. I had never been able to participate in years past because of travel, but now my position had carved out a space for me to work on myself—to work *on* the business of me rather than *in* it, so to speak.

The program involved working closely with a peer study group; over the nine months, I grew close with this group of people, having dinner at one another's houses and getting to know one another very well. We even started to be accountability partners to one another in the process, which included a 360-degree "Reflected Best Self" assessment, where we told stories about one another at what we perceived as one another's best selves.[4]

Prior to this we had been asked where we thought *we* were happiest and most effective. I don't even remember now, but I think my answer at the time was something along the lines of advisory or support roles being where I thought I was at my best. The Reflected

---

4   For more information on this assessment, see https://reflectedbestselfexercise.com/.

Best Self-assessment, though, synthesized what others said about me into an unequivocal answer: others said I was happiest and most effective as a teacher or as a coach.

This was a surprise. I was a finance guy; that was my bread and butter. Saying I was going to be a coach sounded to me like saying I was going to be a poet—I don't know how a poet pays their bills! If I'm going to be a coach, how would I do that and be able to afford the kind of lifestyle I wanted to live? The only reference point I had for that was a sports coach, which I knew wouldn't make sense for me. And a teacher? My mom was a middle school teacher, so I know a lot about the lifestyle and hard work of being a teacher, and I knew I wasn't suited for that.

Still, the more I thought about it, the more sense it made. There was a tug-of-war going on in my mind, and the side that was pulling toward coaching and teaching was winning. I was reorienting how I thought about what coaching means and where it could be practiced. I thought back to my relationship with Rudy Karsan, which I discussed in the introduction, and similar relationships with other CEOs from my private equity days. Sure, I had been their coach. And a lot of the work I had been doing on boards was certainly coaching business leaders, wasn't it?

The next step, then, was to figure out what the call to action was in that feedback. I needed to think about how I could leverage my superpower, my gift for teaching and coaching. More board work would certainly be a great opportunity—I hadn't yet been on a public company board, which I knew would be a great opportunity where I could basically act as a coach at a high level. I decided to get serious about getting on a public company board. Also, since my MBA, I had dreamed of one day going back to teach at HBS. Maybe I should stop treating that like a distant blip on my radar and start doubling down on it as a real potential opportunity.

I knew this reorientation would require some trade-offs and some tough choices, but I started to get excited about it. I had lost the excitement in my CFO work, where I had the big title but hadn't attained my treasure. When I started to get that excitement back, I realized what had happened: I had found my superpower.

Know Yourself

The first step to success on your leadership journey starts with the first ring: yourself. The first two Cs both concern self-knowledge and self-empowerment, first through your superpower (capability) and then through the background and experience you inevitably bring with you into social situations (culture). And the first form of self-knowledge we're going to discuss is knowledge of your *superpower*, which is the heart of the first of the 5 Cs: capability.

You have to know your superpower! Your superpower is the articulation of your unique set of skills and gifts, whether you were born with them or have developed them over time. Whatever your superpower is, *that* is the main thing you have to contribute—whether that is to your own mission or purpose or to that of some organization you are part of. This leads to a self-discovery journey—like my experience with Leadership Atlanta.

The thing that sets you off on your leadership journey may be that where you currently are isn't working for you anymore, however that comes about. That could be external factors—a layoff, for instance—or internal factors—in my case, I was at a career inflection point, because I had achieved a C-suite title after having some success in private equity, and I was still dissatisfied. In either case, this gives you the opportunity and the motivation to step back and take a close look at where you are and where you want to be.

So how do you know what your superpower is? This will be the main topic of the next chapter, but for now, look at my example. As I mentioned, the clue for me was that I started getting excited again. When you're acting on your superpower, it shouldn't feel like drudgery. It should feel exciting. I realized that much of the coaching and teaching work I had been doing—the stuff that was in line with my superpower—was stuff I had been doing on weekend phone calls, or over coffee, for no compensation. Your superpower is that thing that you would do even if you didn't get paid for it; it just comes naturally to you.

Many of us have heard of the Pareto principle: 80 percent of your outcomes result from 20 percent of your activities. The other 80 percent of the time, you're just getting by. Well, what are you doing with that 20 percent of the time? And how do you craft your life around it? How do you flip the switch so that the majority of your time is taken up employing your superpower? For me, the thought was *I've gotta get myself into a classroom and on some public company boards and other coaching platforms.* I needed to put myself in positions where I could have broader reach to global leaders.

A superpower is not your only power—it's not just what you're good at. You may be good at a lot of things, but there are only a few things that you're great at, and that's where your superpower lies. I was good at finance and accounting—very good, and I had a lot of success, thanks to those skills. But that's not my calling, my larger purpose. That lies in capability, which I had to figure out, and did with the help of Leadership Atlanta.

This means that your capability, your superpower, is tied to another big question: your purpose. Fortunately, you don't need to know your purpose in life just yet so you can find your superpower. No, what this means is that you can use figuring out your superpower as a clue to figuring out your larger purpose. What makes you exceptional? Where can you be game-changing? There are plenty of other books written about finding your purpose, so I won't dwell too much on it here, but for many of us, it lies in the impact we can have in our second and third rings—and our superpower is what will allow us to have that impact.

If you do feel that you have a calling, that may be where you want to look to find your superpower. What are you called to do—meaning what do you do in your free time, almost like you can't help but do it?

Now, many superpowers are hard to align to a clear job description. If yours is empathy, you probably won't have much luck searching for that on Monster.com. You have to figure out how to package it in a way that fits into a vocation—either your current one or a different one, and in a traditional way or a creative, nontraditional way.

Often, people don't even appreciate their superpower for what it really is—perhaps they're too close to it to see it. But other people see it. This is what I learned from that feedback in the Leadership Atlanta session—other people saw what I was best at better than I did. And after a while I realized other people had been recognizing my superpower all along, without me noticing. That's how I was getting invited to speaking engagements, guest lecturing opportunities, more board work. For years I was coaching in boardrooms, in classrooms, on phone calls, and out in the field investing—almost like I couldn't say no to these opportunities because I felt called to them. I just didn't recognize them for what they were.

What are the things that people come to you for? Why does your phone ring in the middle of the night or on weekends with someone asking you something? It may not even be something you really think about, because you don't have to work at it—it just comes easily to you. Because when something is really your superpower, you really don't have to strive at it—it's just who you are.

GREG WALTON ON HIS SUPERPOWER

Greg zeroes in on his superpower quickly and illustrates how it can be a soft skill not necessarily correlated with a specific job description:

> My superpower is positively connecting with people. I'm really good about getting to meet people, staying connected, communicating well, following up and really just being a good positive connector, to where people can say like, "Hey man, that dude's authentic. He's not faking the funk. He's legit, he's himself."
>
> I get it from my father. My father's the same way, where you generally know when we come into a room, people hear us, we're cheering everybody up. My son said to me about coaching baseball when I missed a few games—and he's never talked like this—"It's not the same when you're not there." I'm like, "Well you can pick up the slack." He's like, "It's not the same. You're engaged, you're pumping us up, you're coaching us." And I didn't think he was paying attention to any of it.

In Action

You may have skills and talents, but your superpower is not really a superpower until you put it into action. That means that you have to put yourself out there, which is risky—we'll talk more about this when we get to the last of the 5 Cs, confidence, but notice that deciding you have to leverage your superpower when there's no job description out there is kind of like stepping into the abyss. For a lot of folks, this means they'll be pursuing something entrepreneurial, or at least intrapreneurial—building a portfolio career, where you have to create something in order to get where you want to be.

This means a trade-off. I was still pretty financially comfortable in my CFO position, doing a job I knew I was competent at. The path of least resistance would have been just to leave well enough alone—maybe sacrifice a little on the passion and excitement side in order to maintain financial and career security. But if you've read with me this far, my guess is that you're not willing to make that trade-off, or at least you have doubts about it.

So you have to put it into action. I came to believe that teaching and coaching was what I was supposed to be doing. I started referring to myself as a coach. I decided to put it on the line and test it by pursuing a teaching position at HBS. I was very intentional about where I pursued a teaching opportunity. If this is truly my superpower, then I ought to be able to do it at the highest level—one of the best business schools in the world, one where I had dreamed of being able to teach one day. My thought was, *OK, I believe I can do it—can I make someone else believe it too?*

This is a risk—I was exposing myself. I had never taught anywhere. But at the same time, what's the worst that could happen? They say no, and I figure out the next thing. I would just step back and reevaluate—maybe I wanted to teach somewhere else first, or maybe there was another path to HBS. But nothing was stopping me from applying except fear. *The cave you fear to enter holds the treasure you seek.* But you can start by tiptoeing into the cave, seeing if you can rack up some small wins. Applying for the job was my way of tiptoeing into the cave—risky, yes, but not a matter of life and death.

I had been putting this off as something that would happen later when other things had fallen into place—almost as if I was waiting to de-risk the rest of my life before taking this one risk. I was going to wait until I was close to being able to retire and my youngest had gone off to college: if I had gotten the most difficult adulting pieces out of the way, it would be safe again to take the risk, to start thinking about doing this ambitious new thing.

But I was coming to realize that I shouldn't wait, and I didn't need to. If this was my superpower, I should be acting in alignment with it *now*. And I should go all in. Like I said, I was already acting on my superpower on the side, in my free time. I was still active in my network of HBS alums, organizing them, giving guest lectures, judging venture competitions. I was tiptoeing *around* it rather than jumping in with both feet.

You're always going to have an excuse to wait. But once I had pinpointed my superpower, I decided it was time to act. I hadn't even worked out the logistics—I live in Atlanta, and I'd have to be commuting back and forth to Boston! But I decided to take the first step—see if they want me. Gauge their interest. See if I can get the role before worrying about how I'm going to deliver in the role.

This major decision came about because I had taken time to step back and work *on* the business of me rather than *in* it, and I started by locating my superpower, my capability. If you're a sports fan, you've probably heard that great teams are made in the offseason. Well, this time with Leadership Atlanta was my offseason. I was focusing on developing my strengths—including figuring out what my core strength, my superpower, even was—so that I could be more effective when I got back in the game. In the next chapter, we'll dive into how you can start that work too.

TERRI BRADLEY ON HER SUPERPOWER

Like Greg, Terri locates her superpower in the relationships she forges with people:

> I think my superpower is being able to make authentic connections with people. I really do get that from my mom. She never met a stranger. And I believe that people do business with people that they think are competent but also that they like and they trust. I've never been a transactional relationship person … and that has served me well. I think me being able to just be very comfortable in my skin and be who I am and not have to code switch when I'm on the phone … has served me well, and it's been something that has benefited me in my personal and my professional life.

Prompts for Reflection

- What is your superpower? How do you display it?

- If you don't know your superpower yet, what are the three most likely candidates? Why?

CHAPTER 3:

Capability: Your Story

I believe that each of us carries a bit of inner brightness, something entirely unique and individual, a flame that's worth protecting. When we are able to recognize our own light, we become empowered to use it.

—MICHELLE OBAMA

Benedita first showed up in my office hours when she was a student in my intro to finance class. It was still early in the semester, but she was already starting to get nervous about her grade.

"These concepts are just so abstract and foreign to me, I'm getting nervous that I'm not going to be able to truly understand them," she said.

"I'll bet they're not as foreign as they seem. Tell me a little about yourself, Benedita—what's your background, what did you study for undergrad?"

"I went to Johns Hopkins on an engineering scholarship. I'm from São Paulo originally, but I've always been really good with technical things. I was at BCG before coming to school, a strategy consulting internship that turned into a job. I was going to get my masters in engineering, but I saw some of the stuff the other consultants in my cohort were doing and got really excited about an MBA instead."

"What excited you about it?" I asked.

"They were just very entrepreneurial and had cool ideas for businesses. I thought maybe I could do something like start a business back in São Paulo that could help people who come from the same background as me." As soon as she had said this, her nervousness kicked in again, and she got a little tight-lipped. "I don't know; maybe it was a bad idea. I don't know if I'm cut out for that, and I'm not sure I belong here."

I smiled, hoping to put her at ease. "How are you liking Boston? What do you do for fun?"

"It's good; I like the city, though honestly it's still pretty small compared to São Paulo. For fun?" She got a little embarrassed. "I'm a gamer—mostly puzzle-based games, as long as they also have good stories. Like I said, I'm good at figuring out technical problems. And I like the stories too—both in games and writing my own."

"You're a writer?" I asked, surprised.

She laughed. "Not exactly. I did think about being an English major and doing creative writing, but my parents wouldn't have it. I'm a first-generation college student, and they wanted me to pursue something that would get me the best job, so I did the engineering thing."

I wanted to learn more about the business idea that led her to switch from engineering to an MBA, but I didn't want to press too hard in this first conversation, so I went with a softball: "Did you enjoy consulting?"

"Yeah, it was great," she replied, not entirely convincingly. "I had job security, and it's at a firm with a well-known brand, which my parents like. Plus, if I go back and stick around long enough after my MBA, they'll end up paying off my student debt, which is awesome."

"But you're out of your comfort zone a little with the finance stuff," I said. "That's no problem. I'm sure you can figure it out. You certainly have the math skills if you're an engineer. Ever use those skills back in São Paulo before undergrad?"

"Sure; I was on my school's robotics team. I did science fairs and stuff like that. On the more mundane side, I worked at the convenience store that my uncle Antonio owned, and he ended up putting me in charge of managing the money and setting the budget because he knew I could do the math."

I raised my eyebrows. "So finance *isn't* totally foreign to you, is it?"

She laughed. "Well, that's not really the same thing."

"Sure it is," I said. "What you're telling me is that you can totally do this coursework—it just seems like you can't because there's some unfamiliar terminology in there. Sure, it's dressed up in some jargon, and the numbers are bigger, but the fundamentals are the same as managing the finances at your uncle's convenience store. You just want to have more money coming in than going out, right? So you figure out how to minimize costs and make sure you don't run out of money."

"Well, sure, I mean I definitely helped my uncle figure that out—it was fun, like a puzzle."

From here, I was able to direct her back to some of the finance coursework and think of it in those puzzle-solving terms. We worked through a couple of cases together, and she started to rack up some small wins, in that first meeting and in subsequent classes, that started to build her confidence. I coached her as I do many of my students, and she came to realize over time that she was actually good at this finance stuff—she just had to get over being intimidated by some of the unfamiliar jargon.

We bridged the gap by turning the business plans we analyze in the introduction to finance course into puzzles like helping her uncle get his bills paid—she was bright enough to handle the additional complexities that the high finance world introduced. Before, she was helping make sure all of her uncle's employees got paid; now, she was showing how an entire division of Boeing could cover its costs—the same fundamentals were there.

Benedita's creative puzzle-solving ability turned out to be a hidden gem, or better, a hidden key that unlocked her understanding of material that she was struggling with. She had taken this ability for granted, not realizing that it was an asset she could marshal to work in her favor. She had just been using this skill without fully realizing its value. In other words, she had found her *superpower*.

What Is Your Superpower?

With the business owners, founders, and entrepreneurs I advise, I emphasize taking the time to work *on* the business, not just in it. This is a familiar idea for business leaders, but I think the same is true for us personally. Sometimes, though, we get so caught up doing the day-to-day stuff that we need to do to get by—paying the bills, going to work day after day, making sure our taxes are paid, trying to spend time with family—that we don't take that time to work on ourselves. For this reason, I try to emphasize with my business students that their time at business school is not just about learning the course material but is also an opportunity for them to step back and work on their own strengths and abilities, to start developing their leadership capital so that they can be that much more effective when they go back out in the "real world."

I could see already in my first conversation with Benedita that she was setting out on her own leadership journey, starting with unlocking the secret to her *capability*. Mastery of the first of the 5 Cs, capability, requires both identifying and leaning into your superpower. Your superpower, as I explained in the previous chapter, is the articulation of your unique set of skills and gifts, whether you were born with them or have developed them over time. Your superpower will often turn out to be something you don't even recognize as an asset—it just comes so naturally to you, and it's not necessarily something you've intentionally leveraged into fulfilling some job description. But odds are you've been using it all your life in other ways—and other people will recognize it.

Benedita's superpower was what I would call *creative puzzle-solving*—coming up with unique approaches and solutions to puzzles and difficulties. This is why she enjoyed the kinds of games she played and why she excelled at the type of technical work that had gone into her engineering degree. And other people recognized it—she had received recognition all her life for her technical ability, and her uncle had relied on her to help run his business for this very reason. But she was also very creative; this found an outlet in her writing, but I could tell she would be more satisfied if it could play a more prominent role in her work life as well.

Again, your superpower is not necessarily just something you're good at—you may have a lot of skills, and part of the capability journey is continuing to develop the skills that you need to accomplish your goals and pursue your treasure. Still, one of the first steps on your leadership journey is to slow down, step back, and take a look at your talents, gifts, and skills. What are you good at? What are you *great* at?

And among those things, what connects with your sense of passion and purpose enough to qualify as a superpower?

But how do you figure out what your superpower is? Here are some questions you can ask yourself.

WHAT DO YOU DEVOTE YOUR FREE TIME TO?

Your superpower will usually be connected to the thing you *cannot* do—almost like you're compelled. What do you do in your free time? What do you do on your nights and weekends, even though you aren't getting paid for it? As I mentioned in the previous chapter, even while I considered myself a finance guy, I was advising people in my network on their business plans and their careers—coaching them, basically—even though they weren't paying me. I would just do it on long weekend phone calls or over coffee during a break from my other work. It was not just a skill that I had, such as, say, accounting; it was deeply connected to my passion and purpose, which is what made it my superpower.

Benedita's superpower of creative puzzle-solving found an outlet in her preferred leisure activity of gaming. She also wrote stories, giving her another outlet for the creative way she thinks. If you, like Benedita, often find your mind going back to a specific area or thought process (in Benedita's case, *How can I make this work?*), then that may be a clue that you are tapping into something you have a superpower for.

WHAT ARE OTHER PEOPLE TELLING YOU YOUR SUPERPOWER IS?

Seriously: one of the most powerful ways to figure out your super-power is for other people to tell you what it is. People will often see things in you that you don't see in yourself. The Reflected Best Self Exercise that my Leadership Atlanta study group did is designed to coax exactly this type of insight out of other people and present it to you, and this is exactly how I discovered my superpower of coaching and teaching.

In most cases, people won't tell you so directly—though it certainly doesn't hurt to ask the people who know you best or work with you most closely. More often, though, people will give you clues to their superpower by asking certain things of you. Remember, Coach Wycoff saw something in me that I didn't see when he made me quarterback of my peewee football team. And, from my early days as a junior private equity associate, I had both partners and coworkers coming to me for advice on business planning and investment deals. That's how my weekends came to be made up of coffee dates and phone calls (not to mention the occasional cocktail hour). People were asking me to act as a coach even before I realized I was one.

You can find another clue by paying closer attention to the types of compliments you receive—especially the ones you brush off. Maybe a friend shares a difficulty they're having with you and at the end of the conversation says, "Thanks; you're such a good listener." You may think, *Well, of course, I listened—we were talking, and you had something to tell me. What else would I do?* But there's a profound truth in your friend's compliment. Being a good listener is not something that comes easily to most people—maybe this is a place to look for your superpower. It means something to someone else, even though you may say, "Oh, it was nothing." This feeling of it being "nothing" to you leads to our last question.

WHAT FEELS EFFORTLESS TO YOU?

As I've mentioned, when you're acting in alignment with your super-power, it shouldn't feel hard. It should feel natural, even effortless. Others might recognize that, when you are doing this, you are clearly at your best. But you may not recognize it yourself.

You may even get frustrated with other people when they don't share your superpower. Again, you're dismissive of it in yourself, because it comes naturally to you, and you think it should come naturally to everyone. That's why it can be so hard to discern in yourself. So, what do other people do (or not do) that exasperates you?

* * *

The answers to these questions may not come to you easily right away. That's why starting the leadership journey here with capability requires some time taken for introspection. Consider keeping a journal, not necessarily where you try to pour out your deepest thoughts and feelings (not that there's anything wrong with that) but where you just observe yourself for a while. Be a fly on the wall of your own journey. Take note of what activities you kept coming back to because they felt natural, effortless, or like you entered a "flow" state. Note any compliments people gave you or tasks people asked you to do or to help them with. These will be a good guiding light to help you find your superpower.

Discovering your superpower is a very personal journey. There is no one-size-fits-all prescription I can give for figuring it out in a foolproof way. You have to start where you are and work with what you have. The questions are designed to guide you to clues and to increase your likelihood of coming across your superpower—to get you looking in the right places, so to speak. You can seek out coaching or external assessments, too. But at the end of the day, it's up to you to do the introspective brainwork to come to your own discovery.

You can even treat your potential superpower like a scientific hypothesis and find ways to test it out in the world. How do you start applying your superpower or finding ways to lean into it? As I mentioned before, a superpower is not really a superpower until it's put into action or practice in some way. Figuring out how to do this is the next part of the capability journey.

What Do I Do with It?

One tough part of the capability journey is that your superpower will often not be among the types of hard skills that you tend to list on your résumé. It will often be more of a soft skill, such as storytelling, listening, or creative puzzle-solving. For that reason, it might be hard to figure out how to align your superpower with your current career or your career goals—there may not be an obvious job description that matches your superpower. Even if your superpower does tend to align with a particular job, that job may not be within reach for you for external reasons. In my case, coaching and teaching are certainly jobs that people can have, but I needed to start from where *I* was to figure out how to make coaching and teaching opportunities *for me*.

So the challenge is how to apply your superpower. This is one reason people find that they've often been doing it in their free time rather than in what they get paid to do. Their superpower may not be aligned with what they do to pay their bills. Your superpower may not obviously align with what you currently do, and it may not be clear how someone gets paid to do whatever your superpower is. How does a good listener pay the bills? To figure this out, you may need to stretch your understanding of what someone with your superpower can do.

One thing I did was look to examples of people I admire who were exercising my superpowers of coaching or teaching in a context closer to what I did. Dennis Hightower, for instance, was a professor at HBS who came there from the business world, having sat on numerous boards and been a high-ranking executive at Disney. He was certainly doing teaching work, and even his board work likely involved some coaching—again, I was rethinking my own board work as being a type of coaching, so it started to make sense. If he went from that type of work to teaching, maybe I could too.

As you do your introspective work, you may start to discover ways in which your superpower, though not obvious, is actually embedded in what you do, even if it's not in your title or job description. I could find ways in which teaching and coaching had cropped up in my own career. Benedita could point to ways she had applied creative puzzle-solving to her consulting work. Looking for these ways that your superpower is already at work in your life not only helps you visualize a potential path for yourself but also helps you start to build confidence in yourself. You start to tell yourself your own story as a person with that superpower.

This is how I gained the confidence to go for a position at HBS. We'll see in later chapters how Benedita decided to direct her superpower to bring it to fruition, but even identifying it helped her start building confidence—in particular, the confidence to keep on working, and ultimately excelling, at the course material for Finance I.

GREG WALTON ON BENEFITING FROM HIS SUPERPOWER

Greg credits leaning into his superpower for a lot of the success he has had:

> Just being a positive person has taken me places I would've never dreamed of. Literally just, "Hey, how you doing? Good to see you"—just having that energy. I've seen the benefits it's had in my life, and it's not an acting gig, it's just who I am.
>
> My superpower, in a sense, has allowed me to win the highest honor you can win at MIT, an MIT Excellence Award … The [people who nominated me] wrote up a whole nice proposal, not only about the work that I was doing at MIT, but the work with Year Up, the work with going back to speak at high schools to share what I wish I knew, the community work.
>
> Me winning the MIT Excellence Award was a gateway to open up those worlds merging and people appreciating me not for being an IT support engineer, but just for being Greg.

Connecting with Passion

After a few conversations during office hours, I was finally able to get Benedita to admit that she wasn't thrilled with the prospect of going back to her consulting job. She came to realize that she didn't really feel like it was channeling her superpower of creative puzzle-solving in a way she found fulfilling. Her most enjoyable activities from that perspective were things she was doing in her free time, such as gaming and doing other side projects.

"But surely you're doing some creative puzzle-solving in your consulting work, right?" I asked.

"Yeah, it's fun sometimes I guess, and I'm pretty good at it. It pays well. I could keep doing it indefinitely and make a pretty good living. I just keep wondering if there's something else I should be doing."

I could tell that Benedita was missing a crucial piece that would make her capability journey fully come to fruition. She was experiencing a *passion gap*, because there was a mismatch between how she was applying her superpower in her job, on the one hand, and a sense of purpose that would channel her passion, on the other. In the context of consulting with business leaders about operational strategy, her superpower of creative puzzle-solving didn't feel all that super to her.

The key to tapping into your superpower, as I mentioned in the previous chapter, is connecting it up with a sense of purpose. In Benedita's case, she needed to connect her skill set with her passion, which we ultimately determined centered around going back to Brazil to have some positive social impact on her home community. In particular, she was grateful for the educational opportunities she'd had and felt that it was unfair that more kids from poor neighborhoods like the one she came from didn't have access to better educational resources. "If I could choose to have an impact anywhere," she told me, "it would be there: educational opportunity in my home community."

This didn't come out all at once, of course. As it does for many young people in her position, business school was giving her an opportunity to step back and do some introspection and explore some new possibilities. To get to your sense of purpose, you may want to ask yourself what is your (as Jim Collins called it) big hairy audacious goal, or BHAG. This may not be the thing you tell people when they first ask what you want to accomplish—you may be too afraid or embarrassed to say it at first. Even if you do say it, the gap between what you're doing now and where you want to get to may seem so large that it's impossible.

Deep down, Benedita wanted to go back and have positive social impact on people in her community in São Paulo. But she had not figured out exactly how she was going to do that, and the gap between the type of strategic operations consulting she was doing for BCG and what she wanted to accomplish in São Paulo was so large that it discouraged her. She had a severe passion shortfall.

She was doing some puzzle-solving in her consulting role, but so far that had been the only way that she could figure out to make a living doing what she was good at. She had fit her superpower into a commercial role. That's great news, but if the passion is not there, then the journey is not finished. Benedita did not spend her weekends thinking about how to solve operational challenges for Fortune 500 companies but was rather thinking about her family and friends back home and how she could help them with *their* challenges.

There is risk here of course—a trade-off between passion and the practical. Again, you have to start from where you are. It's a personal decision whether you dive into the deep end of pursuing your passion and aligning your superpower to it. But I do think that the people who are the most satisfied with their journey (no matter how successful they are from an external perspective) are those who have taken some of the risk to let go of the side of the pool and dive deeper into their passion.

If you've found your superpower, it can be intimidating to really dive into it. Leaning into your superpower exposes you to risk and makes you vulnerable to an extent. It may not lead you down the route of a safe, nine-to-five job. It led me to a portfolio career. Benedita would have to figure out what path it would lead her down, but as we'll see, it's a path that requires her to step outside of her comfort zone.

Taking these routes might be frightening because we've been, to some extent, institutionalized into sameness—trying to fit what we do into the mold of what everybody else is doing, what others who came before us have done, or what others approve of and think we should do. The idea of differentiating yourself and standing out becomes something we try to avoid. But a leadership journey requires that we lean into what makes us stand out, our superpower.

This is part of Joseph Campbell's message of *The cave you fear to enter holds the treasure you seek*. There may be a big treasure—your BHAG—and a big cave that you have to find your way into in order to find that treasure. But you'll have to enter many little caves to find little treasures along the way, and discovering and leaning into your superpower is the first of these on your leadership journey. You have a hidden talent or gift right in front of you—your superpower; all you need to do is develop the confidence to embrace it and put it to work in service of your passion and your purpose.

Coaching Tips

- Try the journaling exercise I have described in the chapter. For instance, set aside a week during which you'll write down every compliment you receive or every favor someone asks of you, no matter how small. At the end, look at all the examples you wrote down and see if there is some common factor among them that you can use to guide you to your superpower.

- If you have the resources, consider making use of an external skills assessment, such as the Hermann Brain Dominance Instrument (HBDI; see https://www.thinkherrmann.com/hbdi), which assesses how individuals work, think, and communicate at their best.

- Seek feedback from people you are close to or whom you work with on what they think your superpower might be. The Reflected Best Self Exercise (https://reflectedbestselfexercise.com/) is a formal tool for soliciting this type of insight.

- If you've detected a potential superpower, brainstorm ways to test it out in the real world.

- List five people you admire who display your superpower in some way. Look at their career trajectories to see how they leveraged that superpower into pursuing their passion. How might you follow their example?

CHAPTER 4:

Culture: My Story

When you know yourself, you are empowered. When
you accept yourself, you are invincible.

—TINA LIFFORD

I returned to my seat at a professional development event for aspiring young African entrepreneurs in Gambia, where I had just given a presentation on the four Cs of leadership development: capability, communication, connection, and confidence. The woman sitting next to me got up to take my place as the speaker introduced her: Dr. Nzinga Metzger of Florida A&M University. I was surprised when she began by immediately building off my presentation: "I'd like to introduce another 'C' that Mr. Jones did not discuss, but that could be a valuable addition to his framework: culture."

This was actually during my first visit to West Africa; I was making the trip to build the network for my coaching and do some speaking engagements, but more importantly, I was looking to make closer contact with my culture. It is just by coincidence that I encountered and connected with a woman, a fellow teacher who lived only a state

57

away from me, when we were both on the other side of the Atlantic—and she taught me as much about culture as anyone else, starting with that presentation where she gifted me the fifth of the 5 Cs.

"I was put on the spot that day," Nzinga, who is now a good friend, later told me.[5] "I was supposed to be attending that event with someone who got ill and sent me by myself, and I thought I was going as an audience member." She was taken aback when an event organizer welcomed her by saying, "We can't wait to hear you speak!" She was going to have to speak to a room of over a hundred young people, and she wasn't entirely sure what the event was even about.

As an anthropologist, Nzinga said, "I just had to fall back on my own knowledge base, because ... I don't know business school jargon or anything like that, but what I do know is culture. Basically, what I talked about that day was the importance of this particular contingent of students taking their culture into the workplace with them as they move forward and try to become relevant in these Fortune 500 and Fortune 100 companies."

Indeed, these entrepreneurs would take her lessons into many organizations, large and small, that are working to transform Africa. Nzinga argues that, after centuries of colonial exploitation, Africa is beginning to play a more self-determined role in the global economy, with a very young population pushing for new opportunities. Her message that day was powerful: "The only way that Africa and Africans have a chance at successfully navigating Africa's new role in the next hundred years is if Africans really begin to take themselves to task on some of the values that they've internalized over the past few centuries, many of which have denigrated and devalued indigenous African thinking, indigenous African systems, indigenous African values."

---

5   All quotes from Dr. Metzger are from an interview conducted on March 24, 2023.

In other words, she wanted these young people to shift their understanding of their own cultural background and roots, from being a liability to being an asset that can add value both for them and for the organizations they are a part of. In particular, Dr. Metzger highlighted indigenous African traditions that emphasized the development of people into decent and humane adults who are part of a family and community. If these young people could bring a focus on personal development and connection into game-changing organizations, they could find success themselves and do it in a way that benefited everyone, from their second ring out into their third ring.

Dr. Metzger remembers how she felt watching my presentation and frantically trying to figure out what she was going to say: "I remember having this feeling like, 'Wow, I never thought about having the conversation he's having with these young entrepreneurs-to-be,' and I … remember feeling a certain level of joy at the potential for them to be inspired and to feel like they have an opportunity there." She then leaned into her own superpower, which for her *is* her culture, and came out with an authentic and powerful message that spoke to these young people. Seeing herself as part of a shared culture with the audience took away her fear at not having any remarks prepared.

I was wowed by Dr. Metzger's speech. Culture has certainly been a part of my own leadership journey, and it has been part of the leadership capital framework since that day. It follows directly on capability as being a crucial part of the introspection, self-knowledge, and self-empowerment that the leadership journey requires.

What Is Culture?

Culture, as Dr. Metzger describes it, goes deeper than styles of clothing, music, food, and dance, to include entire sets of values and ways of thinking: "What emphasis do you put on relations between people? How are you supposed to relate to people? How are you supposed to relate to the planet? How are you supposed to speak?" She defined culture to me as "the symbol system—learned, shared, and passed down from generation to generation—behind the assumptions you make about the world. It gives you your template for interpreting the world and communicating with it."

In the terms of the leadership capital framework, culture as the second of the 5 Cs involves understanding your unique background, values, and perspective on the world and leveraging those things to make your unique contribution. As I have discussed in the previous chapter, we often feel like the safest route is to blend in, to assimilate, not to stand out. Many people have a "work self," and they check their *whole* self at the door of their workplace. Everyone struggles with this to some extent. For people from marginalized populations, such as people of color or people from the LGBTQ+ community, this sense of feeling the need to assimilate can be especially strong—and especially damaging. We all need to resist viewing our culture this way. Just as we did with our capability, we need to come to realize that our culture is something to be openly embraced.

The culture journey involves coming to value who you uniquely are and leveraging your uniqueness to build confidence and drive success. This is easier said than done, of course. Through discriminatory practices and negative stereotypes, many other people still do show that (consciously or not) they do not value certain people's cultural backgrounds. Just because they do not value it, though, does not mean it isn't *valuable* and that you can't see the value in it yourself. You've got to know your own worth before someone else can come to know it. Whoever you are, lean into it and work to become more comfortable in your skin and with your own culture that you bring to every situation.

If you pull a diamond out of your pocket, but the person you're showing it to doesn't recognize it as a diamond, that doesn't make it any less valuable. If they refuse to believe that it's a diamond, then that is their problem, not yours, and you may be better off going to show the diamond to someone else. The worst mistake you can make in the face of that other person is to start undervaluing the diamond yourself. Not everyone is going to recognize the value of your culture and heritage right away, and that's fine. The culture journey is about building the confidence to recognize and insist on that value yourself.

TERRI BRADLEY ON IMPOSTER SYNDROME

Terri strongly states the importance of bringing your whole, authentic self to the table:

> You've got to just be authentic and true to yourself. I think most people appreciate that. And if I'm not somebody's cup of tea, that's OK too. I think that's where people fail themselves. I'm going to show up, I'm going to be me, and I'm going to be all of me. I tell women all the time, "Take up all your space" … You are there, because you deserve to be there.
>
> I've never dealt with imposter syndrome. It's never been a thing for me. I'm in a room because I deserve to be in the room, and it makes no sense for me to go in the room and try to be a chameleon and act like everybody else in the room, because that's not how I got in the room in the first place. So where someone else may be a little more delicate or be a little bit more humble or whatever else, that's their role. That's how they got in the room. That's not me. I think part of that is just when

you come through the storm, how can you show up anything less … You might be weathered and worn, but you're there.

I think for people who struggle with imposter syndrome, oftentimes it's because you don't believe people. You don't believe you should be in the room. So it's a matter of *What do you have to unlearn? What do you have to stop telling yourself?* Because it's not even usually all the outside voices—it's just your own inner voice that makes you struggle with imposter syndrome. And so whatever they're saying doesn't really matter, because the person who's saying the cruelest thing is you, saying it to yourself. And you've got to be able to say something new to yourself.

Tapping into My Culture

I had to make some progress on my own culture journey when I started teaching at HBS. This was my first time teaching in any capacity, and my first semester happened to be the spring semester of 2020—the COVID spring when lockdowns changed the lives of almost everyone on the earth. I had only a handful of opportunities to meet and present myself to my students face-to-face before the whole affair got pushed online. I was making my first attempt at trying to understand how to lead a classroom, and I didn't even *have* a real classroom.

My teaching evaluations that semester left a lot to be desired, which was a blow to my confidence. I couldn't blame it all on COVID, though. As it was my first semester, I did my best to teach strictly according to the teaching plan I had been given for the courses I was teaching. These teaching plans can act basically like a script—but getting up in front of a (real or virtual) class and *reading a script* can be a trap. Because this is what I was doing, I wasn't bringing myself to my teaching much at all. A fellow professor and mentor helped me realize that my students weren't seeing the *real Archie*, the one who engaged so well outside of class. Over time, though, I've gained enough familiarity with the teaching plans that I can actually depart from them more, and as I've gained that freedom, I'm able to inject myself more and more into my teaching. I weave in my own stories, sharing the challenges I've faced and the lens through which I view them because of my own cultural background.

I've also brought my own personality more into my teaching. It helped me to remember the words of one of my advisors from Morehouse College: "Archie, you can't pretend to be someone you're not when you enter a room. You're an open, approachable leader—so be that!" This teacher's advice—which sums up so much of what we all need to learn on our culture journeys—led me to a more authentic presentation of myself in the classroom. Since then, I can proudly say my teaching evaluations have soared, but more importantly, my approach has started to resonate with students so that the Beneditas in the class seek me out outside of the classroom.

In fact, one of my colleagues who is a couple of years behind me on his teaching journey recently asked me to sit in on one of his classes and give him some feedback. He had heard through the grapevine that some of his students weren't happy. I happily obliged, and when I watched him, I saw exactly what I probably looked like back in the spring of 2020. I knew this man as, like me, a gregarious guy with a big personality, but here he was standing stiffly behind a lectern, one hand in his pocket, and following the script so tightly that he was losing the connection with the students in the room.

Some professors stay behind the lectern and are soft-spoken, and the class gets quiet because the students are being attentive, and that works for that teacher because that's who they authentically are. I, on the contrary, am loud, and I'm on the move—I'll walk up and down the alleyways of the auditorium-style seats. I make the class my own. I think those different approaches can both work because, in both cases, students can sense the teacher's authenticity and find it inherently compelling.

Some of the required first-year classes have ten professors teaching them to groups of eighty-plus students each, and we meet with one another to work out a game plan of what we're going to cover to make sure we're covering the same bases. Within that, we're each given freedom as to how we present the material.

I run my class like a board meeting—just another way of bringing my own background into my teaching. I put our three main agenda items on the board, and then I pick a lineup of three students who will start the discussion of each item like it's their agenda item in a meeting. Now, the student who gets the first agenda item gets put on the spot a little bit, but I still give them a few minutes at the beginning of class to prepare remarks, and all they're really there to do is get the discussion started based on the materials provided.

I know what key elements of the teaching plan I have to hit on, but apart from that, I entirely make up the board meeting format. It just feels like a natural way to run a business school class for me from a professional culture perspective, both in the sense of what I am used to and in the sense of what would best prepare them to go out into the business world. And the students love it. It makes them comfortable, I'm comfortable, and it gives a sense of order and organization to what can really be a pretty freewheeling discussion about a business case study we're examining. It helps to put three rings around the circus—otherwise you've just got clowns and animals running around.

Again, no one taught me this method; I just developed it organically. And when I first presented it to the other professors, it caused some raised eyebrows: "You seriously do this every time?"

"Yeah, that's what I do—and it works for me."

Some of them may be skeptical, because it's further afield from the script or teaching plan that we all follow, but they also see the results in my teaching evaluations. And I don't think that's because it's a superior format—there's a good chance it wouldn't work as well for another professor who wasn't as comfortable with the board meeting format as I am. There are other professors at HBS with completely different styles who are still award-winning teachers. Again, whatever the style is, students appreciate it when it's authentic.

Like capability, the culture journey is going to be individualized, and you have to start from where you are. You may need to spend some time following the norms before you become comfortable stepping out of them. There's truth in the old saying, "You have to know the rules before you can break the rules (or make new ones)." I had to get that script down pretty well before I was comfortable diverging from it. It's OK to take some time making that part of the journey. But it was when I did diverge and start bringing myself to it that I started being most effective as a teacher. As Dr. Metzger predicted for the young entrepreneurs she was speaking to, me bringing myself and my culture to my teaching led to the best outcome for everyone.

Like devaluing my own diamond, the worst mistake I could have made in the face of bad teaching evaluations was to try *harder* to fit the mold, follow the script, or teach the way other professors did. At that point, I'm moving away from both my culture and my capability, things are getting harder, and outcomes are getting worse. It's ultimately an unsustainable approach.

Still, taking this first step on the culture journey—shifting your mindset from thinking of your heritage or the culture you grew up in as a liability to thinking of it as an asset that has just been hidden up to now, such as a diamond—is easier said than done. In the next chapter, we'll dive deeper into some ways of tackling this mindset shift and leveraging your culture.

GREG WALTON ON HIS CULTURAL HERITAGE

Greg gives credit to his great-grandmother, who raised him for part of his early childhood, for instilling service in him as a cultural value that has stayed with him:

> Some of the culture that I was able to develop on just how to function as an adult was from my great-grandmother. She was born in the 1910s, so she lived through some stuff, and she actually lived to over a hundred … She was very service oriented. By the time I'm living with her at six or seven years old, she's a spouse to my great-grandfather, who's old, in declining health, and starting to have dementia. And a huge chunk of her time is catered toward just serving and taking care of him.
>
> And sometimes that culture is being built without saying anything, without any direct, verbal communication. I'm visually seeing that. And then … I'm actually a part of that culture of service: I'm cutting his toenails, I'm putting Gold Bond powder on his back, and I'm learning those things at a very early age …
>
> I'm still carrying that service focus from the early parts of that journey, and then here you go with the representation of that: I win my MIT Excellence Award in the *Serving the Client* category. Can't make that stuff up.

Prompts for Reflection

- Think about your cultural background, whether that's race, ethnicity, nationality, religious tradition, or something else.

- Does it have aspects that feel like liabilities or obstacles to success? Why do you think you or others feel this way?

- What elements of your personality do you feel like you have to hide in certain social or professional situations? Why do you feel this way?

- The culture journey discussed in the next chapter involves recasting these liabilities as assets and embracing your uniqueness.

CHAPTER 5:

Culture: Your Story

Our history is our power ... Life will test you, and when it does,
your history will give you the power to meet the challenge.

—MARYLAND GOVERNOR WES MOORE

About midway through her first semester, I approached Benedita in the hallway after class. Her Finance I coursework was going well since she had developed more confidence with it, but I wasn't hearing from her enough in class. I had tried to draw her out a bit by calling on her to cover the last of the three major points we were covering in class that day—a diagnostic of the long-term financial health of the company whose business plan we had been discussing.

"You're getting comfortable with the class material now," I said, "but remember, class participation is fifty percent of your grade. You nailed your part of the presentation today, but I need some more quantity to go with that quality, if you know what I mean. I want to see your hand come up on its own. Why aren't we hearing from you more?"

THE TREASURE YOU SEEK

I knew the answer boiled down to a lack of confidence, but I needed to get Benedita to confront that in order for her to move forward on her journey.

"I know," she said. "It's just really hard in a room of nearly a hundred people to work up the guts to speak up, especially when everybody is so smart and well-prepared."

"You've been doing the work. Don't you feel prepared for class?"

"That's not what I mean," she answered, acting a bit embarrassed.

"Here, let's go back to my office." I thought she might feel more comfortable without her classmates milling around us.

Once she settled in, she said, "I feel prepared on a day-to-day basis, but less prepared in, like ..." She struggled to find the words: "... in a *bigger* sense. Like prepared for all of this." She waved her hand around to indicate what she meant: HBS, an MBA program, the business world. "They were set up for this world, and I'm still having a hard time feeling like I belong here."

I recognized the symptoms of imposter syndrome—despite her stellar academic and early career success, Benedita felt out of place. I knew that, actually, a lot of students felt that way, but from her perspective, they all looked prepared and comfortable. Everyone puts their best face to the world, so sometimes you can only see other people's strengths, while in private you can see your own weaknesses.

"Well, you certainly belong here—you've had numerous job recruiters, admissions people, and Harvard professors tell you that. What's holding you back?"

Benedita unfurled a list of what she saw as liabilities: her accent and English as a second language (ESL) status, her gender, and most of all, her socioeconomic background. "It feels like my section is all high-achieving rich kids, while I'm from the wrong side of the tracks."

I acknowledged that the first year of an MBA program at Harvard could be an intimidating environment. But I also assured her that everyone else was not as put together or buttoned up as she might think. "Lots of students feel this way, no matter what background they're from. You just don't see it. And as for the 'rich kid' thing, yes, there are a lot of folks from privileged backgrounds here, but not all of them are. Plus, don't you think that's actually a point in your favor? You got here purely on the basis of your own competence and hard work, not because of family connections, or because you were set up in the best schools from day one."

I encouraged her to shift her mindset from thinking of all these factors—which add up to the second of the 5 Cs, culture—as liabilities to thinking of them as *assets*. In her culture, I explained, she could find hidden resources that she could draw on to drive her success instead of obstacles that were holding her back.

"I just don't fit in, and I'm kind of freaking out now because I know that so much of what I'm supposed to be doing here is building a social network," she said.

"That will come in time," I reassured her. "And the things that you think are keeping you from fitting in are going to be exactly the things that *set you apart*, that allow you to bring a unique contribution to the table that will make *you* a valuable part of the networks your classmates are building. The first thing you need to do is to start digging into what those differentiators are. You need to start thinking about your *culture*."

A Double-Edged Sword

For most of us, culture is going to be a double-edged sword. We may be proud of some aspects of it and draw on it for confidence, but other aspects of it may hold us back or be an obstacle to developing that confidence. The difference in the role culture can play for us—whether it's something that holds us back or something that propels us forward—is determined by the mindset we take toward it. Sometimes the very thing that seems like an obstacle will be an advantage if we shift our perspective on it.

Benedita, for instance, saw her socioeconomic background as someone from a working-class family in São Paulo as an obstacle to her success at HBS and beyond. With work, though, she came to acknowledge that her experiences back home had endowed her with a resilience and grit that some of her classmates might not have. From that perspective, a classmate who was born with a silver spoon in their mouth and has had their path to HBS laid out for them is going to have a disadvantage when it comes to encountering situations of adversity. They'll react very differently the first time a tough situation knocks them on their ass, so to speak—they may not get back up as easily as Benedita can.

I also pointed out to her that, if her goal really was to have impact on the educational needs of kids back in São Paulo, then she would be a valuable asset to any organization that shared that mission. She was close to the difficulties and knew what they were; she would have valuable insight and connection to the people in the community—an advantage that came directly from her culture.

The first step of the culture journey is to do some introspection and maybe some investigation into what elements of your culture may be holding you back. As I continued to work with Benedita, for instance, I learned that she carried a heavy weight of familial expectations, which is common among students who are the first in their family to go to college or graduate school. She had achieved a certain level of status and prestige that, from her parents' perspective, was the goal, and the safety and security of holding on to that position was going to act as a counterweight to her taking any risks. Their goal by the time she had made it to BCG and Harvard was for her to be upwardly mobile in a renowned organization, and they didn't see this kind of success as possible in her old neighborhood. This mindset, understandably, favors the safety of the practical option over the riskiness of following a personal passion.

However, she could also look to these same familial expectations and family heritage for motivation and support for pursuing her passion. She had already achieved great things from her family's perspective, so she could use this as a confidence booster to help her move out of her comfort zone in new ways. She could also draw on her family's culture of hard work, risk-taking, and entrepreneurship as support for her sense of mission and purpose. So, even as you're finding things in your culture that hold you back, you will discover things that can propel you forward if you approach them with the right mindset.

Most people can go at least a generation or two back in their family history and find stories they can draw on as part of their cultural confidence—and again, these may be a double-edged sword. There may be stories of failure, harm, or bad decisions. But the flip side of each of these is a story of recovery, resilience, courage, and grit to do what it takes to survive and pass life on to a new generation. We can all, at the very least, draw on a legacy of survival from generation to generation.

In my work with Year Up, I've coached young aspiring professionals from difficult backgrounds, many of whom have experienced homelessness and other life-changing challenges growing up. That is something no young person should have to go through, but I have seen some of these young people transform that experience into a source of strength. A challenge or setback in the workplace that might derail some young professionals is not going to knock someone who has been through housing difficulties for as much of a loop. They have the strength of perspective.

In my own case, I can look directly to my parents to think about the roots of my own journey. My father was an entrepreneur, and my mother was a teacher, so both these things are part of my cultural DNA. Going back a bit further, my grandfather farmed and worked construction. My grandfather did this work to provide for his family. He even built the house my father grew up in with his own hands. Now I don't have a handy bone in my body, so some of his capabilities did not get passed down to me! However, I do have a work ethic and a motivation to provide for my family. My grandfather was a provider above all else, which is a heritage he passed down to my father, an entrepreneur, who then passed it on to me.

Even this is a double-edged sword. Some men of older generations who were providers first and foremost may also have passed down a heritage of not being present or emotionally available for their kids. My friend Nzinga Metzger has an important insight here for anyone thinking critically about their cultural heritage:

> Knowing and understanding and appreciating your culture isn't just falling in love with and hailing and extolling the great aspects of your culture. It's also understanding the dysfunctional parts of your culture and deciding, *yeah, I don't agree with that and that's not something that I want to carry into the future.* It's a part of what we come from or where I come from, but it doesn't work or it's dysfunctional or it's wrong ... and that is a part of understanding and moving forward.

My father was a hardworking man and an entrepreneur, whom I saw going out into the community and confidently communicating and networking in order to grow his business and deliver opportunities for the community. This certainly informed my trajectory.

I also grew up seeing my mother as a teacher who spent her own money outfitting her classroom to make it as safe, welcoming, and educational for her students as she possibly could. I would spend a lot of time in the summers helping her decorate her classroom, which she turned into a kind of haven for her students. This was her way of being a *coach*, in the sense of my acronym: *creating opportunity and cultivating humanity*. Her legacy informs much of my work and my mission today as a teacher and coach.

TERRI BRADLEY ON ADVERSITY AS A CULTURAL ASSET

Terri credits the challenges of her youth for some of her current strengths:

> I think all of that makes me who I am today: being a little Black girl growing up in St. Paul, Minnesota, in the seventies, being a child of parents who … got married at sixteen years old and then just tried to figure out how to parent and how to be adults … So that came with a whole level of challenges and dysfunction … I think those adversities made me an empathetic person, made me a stronger person.
>
> I was eleven or twelve years old, taking a city bus from St. Paul to Minneapolis. And if I had to call somebody, I had to use a payphone. And so it made me curious. It made me more adventurous. It made me less afraid of anything … I had to figure out my own transportation. So it made me be a person who knows I can count on myself.

I think there's skills that I would not have cultivated, had I had a very soft life. Do I want a soft life now? Yes! But I would not be where I am or doing what I'm doing, I wouldn't have the fortitude, I wouldn't have the stick-to-it-tiveness and all of that, had I not had the upbringing that I had.

Household and Heritage

The household you grow up in can form a huge part of your culture in both positive and negative aspects. It's not the only part of your culture, though, and it doesn't determine your path. I have three sons who grew up in the same house, eating the same food, going to the same school, and sometimes even wearing the same clothes—and they couldn't be more different from one another. In your case, your upbringing may have left you with some harmful or dysfunctional parts of your culture, but that doesn't mean you can't draw on your experiences—perhaps even just surviving a tough situation—as sources of strength so that you can leave the bad parts behind or use them to your advantage.

The history that shapes part of your own culture and that you can draw on as a resource may also stretch well beyond the last couple of generations and even beyond your own family history. I'm not directly related to Harriet Tubman, but she is certainly someone I have looked to as a cultural hero, and I have worked to internalize and lean into the strengths and the values that she represents to me as a Black American. Less distantly, Reginald Lewis was the first African American to build a billion-dollar business, and it was his example that initially inspired me to want to go into private equity. Before I learned about him, I didn't even know that world existed. He was a man from a culture very similar to mine, who looked like me, who had accomplished incredible things in that world, and it opened up a whole new world of possibilities to me.

Cultural heroes like these can be guideposts for you on your culture journey. Who else from your cultural background do you admire, whose example you can draw on for strength, inspiration, or motivation? If you're not sure, do some research: look online, ask a trusted adviser, look out into your immediate community. This may take some effort, but it will pay off in terms of advancement along your culture journey.

As with all parts of the leadership journey, the culture journey will be different for everyone; it is highly individualized. The weight of household versus broader heritage can vary widely depending on both your upbringing and your cultural background. If your own household upbringing carries too much negative baggage, you may need to counterbalance that with a deep dive into your broader cultural background. If your heritage has aspects you're not particularly proud of, you may draw more on lessons your parents taught you about transcending that background and being a good person. It all depends on what aspects of each you can draw on to serve you and give you strength.

The main question is what you want to get out of your engagement with culture. What it needs to do is propel you forward on your leadership journey, not hold you back. Which aspects of your culture help you build confidence to pursue your passion and sense of purpose? While this journey is individualized, I am confident that this is true for everyone: you can find these things in your history. No matter where you're from, what your lineage is, you can look to your family history and cultural touchstones and conclude that there are assets to be found there. Not everyone may see and recognize those things as assets; that's a separate challenge, which we'll talk about shortly. But the first part of the culture journey is to have the conviction that you can draw on culture to support you and move you forward to success, whatever success means to you.

Your Cultural Balance Sheet

Like Benedita, you may find it easy to rattle off the list of negatives about your culture—the baggage, the stereotypes, the obstacles. As a tool for starting to rethink these negatives, for rewiring your understanding of yourself and your culture, I encourage you to draw up a *cultural balance sheet*.

Bear with me while my inner accounting nerd comes out a bit. A balance sheet tries to graphically balance *assets* on one side with *liabilities and equity* on the other side. The sheet balances by showing that your assets are equal to your equity plus your liabilities. Or, put slightly differently, your *equity*—that excess that belongs to you and that you have available to invest or borrow against moving forward— amounts to the *difference* between your assets and liabilities.

Think about it like having a mortgage on your home. As a homeowner, you have an asset that's worth a certain amount: the value of your home. That value is equal to the combination of what you still owe on the house and the equity you have in the house based on previous payment (or appreciation of the value of the home). If you owe the exact value of the house—if your liability is equal to the value of the asset, then your equity is at zero. Ideally, you owe less than the value of the house, and the amount to which the asset is worth more than you owe is your equity in the house.

On your cultural balance sheet, you want to generate some cultural equity that you can leverage to move forward on your leadership journey. In order to do this, you need your cultural assets to outweigh your cultural liabilities.

When we first start filling out our cultural balance sheets, as I've mentioned, it's natural to start with the liabilities column, like Benedita was doing. The problem is that if you let the liabilities tell your whole story, you end up with an imbalance. To go back to the mortgage analogy, this is like owing more on your home than the home is worth—being upside down on your mortgage, in other words. Then you end up with negative equity in your account.

This is a bad place to be with a mortgage, and the same goes when it comes to your cultural balance sheet. If you leave yourself with a cultural equity deficit, you encounter major obstacles to your leadership journey, such as imposter syndrome or an inferiority complex. You perceive yourself as not belonging, or as not having positive attributes that you uniquely bring to the table.

In that case, as your cultural accountant, I advise you to get rid of some of that liability and increase the value in your asset column. Fortunately, in telling anyone's full story, it's possible to fill out the asset side of the sheet. This is where you look to the positive aspects of your culture, your background and upbringing. Eventually, you need to realize that your assets *outweigh* your liabilities, which is how you end up with some residual equity back on the right-hand side. Once you have a surplus in your cultural equity account, you have some capital to invest moving forward.

Going from deficit to abundance, drawing on both your superpower and your cultural assets, means that you have some capital that you can draw on confidently. This gives you confidence to go out and show that you have something to bring to the table.

Crucially, you can even look to the liabilities side for the hidden gems that you can count as assets. Again, it may be easy to think of liabilities, but these may contribute to your drive and tenacity. With Benedita, for instance, she listed her socioeconomic background as a liability—she came from a relatively poor background in contrast to her (in her perception) privileged classmates. However, this same background gives rise to grit and resilience and could even be linked to entrepreneurial capability, as in the case of her uncle who ran a convenience store. The essence of entrepreneurship is getting a lot done with a little bit of resources, and Benedita could find that cultural asset in her own background. As with Benedita, your perceived liabilities can also be put on the balance sheet as hidden assets on your leadership journey.

I have a whiteboard in my office for doing these types of exercises with students, and I drew up a cultural balance sheet for Benedita. "Oh no, not more accounting," she moaned.

I laughed. "Don't worry, you won't have to crunch too many numbers on this one. So what were those liabilities you were talking about?" I asked.

She listed some of the things we already talked about: her accent and ESL status and her socioeconomic background. "You're bilingual and have a perspective from the global South, which is valuable; and we already talked about the grit, resilience, and entrepreneurship that come from your socioeconomic background," I said, adding assets to go with each of her perceived liabilities.

"I'm a first-generation college student," she said.

I gave her a puzzled look. "Is that supposed to be a liability?"

"Yeah! I'm in class with people who went to Harvard, whose parents and grandparents went to Harvard, and they've been groomed for this world and know how to play the game, and I just haven't," she said.

"OK, fair enough," I said, making a note in the liability column, "but I'm also going to add some things to the asset column about the work ethic your parents handed down to you that made it possible to get into college; the lifestyle, culture, and educational experiences you were exposed to growing up in Brazil that a relatively sheltered white American young person won't encounter; and most importantly, the unique perspective that you bring as a first-generation college student. You can look through a different lens at each of these things you're putting in the liability column, in particular because they make up the unique perspective and outlook that you bring to the table. These are where your contribution is going to come from."

This exercise helped Benedita start to reframe how she was looking at her place in the classroom and in the professional world. From there we were able to start working on her confidence both in the classroom and in other professional contexts, such as networking among her classmates. She had taken the first steps of the culture journey: introspection and reprogramming her understanding of her culture from a set of liabilities to a set of assets.

Now, this may just seem like I'm encouraging you to look at things through rose-colored glasses. This is not the case. I don't mean to tell you that everything you've been through, every trauma or difficulty, is just fine and dandy and that there is nothing holding you back. The key, though, is to realize that those things aren't the whole story; they are just a small part of a larger story, even though in many cases, the story we're telling ourselves is all liability. You need to recognize the other side of the balance sheet and put more weight in the asset category than in the liabilities so that you can generate some equity.

It's also worth remembering that everyone has something in the liability column. This is universal; it's not unique to you or to just one group of people. The next step on the culture journey is to figure out how to quiet the negative aspects, the liabilities, and turn up the volume on the positive aspects, the assets, in order to get your inner voice speaking to you in a way that lifts you up instead of tearing you down. The story you need to tell yourself about culture is about the unique contribution that you bring to the table, and you need to learn to leverage that story for success.

GREG WALTON ON GAINING CONFIDENCE FROM ADVERSITY

Greg exemplifies how tough circumstances can form a cultural backdrop that can be a source of confidence moving forward:

> I was in the foster care system very early. I bounced around homes. I lived with my great-grandmother, then with a great aunt. And I didn't have a lot of stability growing up, even well before going to jail …
>
> One of the first memories of joining Year Up is that they do such a good job of building a sense of community among the students you're with on the journey and really galvanizing you as a group to really realize a greater goal: *Hey, we're all in this journey of trying to be successful young adults and getting careers and really thriving.* And in that space, it really helped me realize I shouldn't feel a lack of confidence to not be able to share my story. I'm a God-fearing man. I certainly believe God had me go through it for a reason to be a beacon, to prove that we can come from anything …
>
> I was [in Year Up] with peers who dodged bullets to get across the border. So we're all connected in a culture that said, "Man, we can do *this*. We got this." And then you fast-forward

> to now, I have to go provide support for professors who have
> won the highest of the highest awards in their field, and I'm not
> nervous. I don't lack confidence going to that space because I
> know what I'm doing, I know I've been through a lot.

Leaning into Difference

One of the goals of shifting our mindsets this way, of starting to
tell ourselves a different story about assets instead of liabilities, is to
combat a major opponent of the culture journey: imposter syndrome.

Imposter syndrome applies to people who have had some measure
of success, who have pursued some goal and achieved it but who still
feel undeserving for whatever reason. They've shown up in the room
they were trying to get into, whether that's literally a classroom or a
boardroom, or just some other metaphorical room—but now that
they're there, they feel like they don't belong.

Imposter syndrome imposes a kind of pressure that is an obstacle
on your leadership journey: the pressure to fit in, to fade into the
background, and to cover up what you uniquely bring to a situation,
instead of trying to fit yourself into the mold that you perceive
everyone else as representing. You want to be comfortable in the room,
so you try to look and act like everyone else in the room.

If we think back to our forms of capital, we can say that you have
as much *experiential* capital as the other people in that room do, but
for whatever reason, you perceive yourself as lacking some experiential
capital that they have. Hence the term *imposter syndrome*, which goes
with the feeling of not belonging, of being in a world that isn't *for
you* somehow.

To some degree, the risk of imposter syndrome and the pressure
to assimilate to a dominant culture is universal, but this feeling can

be particularly strong for people from minority or underrepresented identities. When you look around the room and don't see anyone else who looks like you, the desire *not* to stand out really kicks in.

If this sounds familiar to you, remember my example from the previous chapter of the diamond. Your culture is your diamond, and like a diamond it has been shaped by its history of pressure and struggle. The first steps of the culture journey were about you learning to recognize it as a diamond and to recognize its value. Now we're trying to build the confidence to show off your diamond, so to speak, in the face of an audience who you think won't recognize its value. Keeping the value of your diamond in mind, not devaluing it, is an ongoing task, and the fear of having light shined on it may cause you to keep it hidden. Too often, we hide what makes us different, what makes us stand out. The world can sometimes tell you that, if you want to be in this room, you need to be like the other people in the room. You need to look like them, dress like them, eat what they eat, and go to the same schools they go to.

But the fact of the matter is that what makes you unique is exactly what's valuable. As a group made up of unique individuals, the collective, so to speak, needs different contributions from different folks in order to function effectively. That's why your culture is an asset. The group needs your diamond, whether they realize it at first or not! The group—whether it's your community, your class, an organization whose mission you are a part of, or something else—actually gets stronger when you bring what is valuable and worth sharing from your culture (the assets on your balance sheet) to the party.

Now, let's be honest: I recognize that all of this is easier said than done. Sometimes the people in power are the ones who don't see the value of your diamond, and getting them to recognize it is hard work. I saw this in my own career as a Black man on Wall Street. I had to work twice as hard as some of my colleagues to get recognition, but once I was in the door, I knew my value, and I ended up outperforming a lot of those other folks. It can be a tough climb, but what I don't want to happen is for that tough climb to make you start questioning the value of your culture. A diamond is still a diamond, and at some point, at the right organization at the right time, when you present it in the right way, it will be recognized for its value and highly rewarded.

If you're from a minority or an underrepresented group, you may find yourself assimilating to a certain professional culture, for instance, to make yourself and the others in the room with you more comfortable. You shouldn't beat yourself up about this, in spite of what I've been saying about bringing yourself to the party. It may be helpful, even necessary, as a strategy at first. It may help get you in the room and get comfortable being there. But once you're there, this strategy's effectiveness will be short-lived, and it won't actually get you where you ultimately want to go, operating with your superpower and pursuing your passion and purpose.

Leaning into my culture at HBS has actually led me to some very exciting opportunities. To give an example: the fact of the matter is that, in the world of venture capital and private equity, entrepreneurs of color don't receive anywhere near a proportionate level of access to investment dollars. Some of the other professors in my teaching group struggle with how to present this issue, and there is some discomfort around discussing what they see as a sensitive topic. I, however, have no discomfort talking about it, because I've lived it—I can speak firsthand about it. I also don't hesitate to ask students of color to weigh in with their opinion on the issue, while some professors would struggle with how to approach that.

By bringing this perspective to the table, I've been able to turn an aspect of my culture that many would see as a liability into an asset;

my firsthand experience with discrimination puts me in a position of authority on this topic. As a result, I had the privilege of cofounding two courses focused on working with minority-owned businesses. In one of them, Scaling Minority Businesses, we discuss not only how enterprise is a tool that disadvantaged people can use to their advantage but also how capitalism has been intertwined with racism throughout its history. Other professors might feel uncomfortable discussing some of these issues, but I have been able to make it into a successful course where students are doing some valuable work in the community. I would not have had that opportunity but for my cultural background—the unique experiences, relationships, and per-spectives that I bring to the table. I had only been at HBS a year or so when this opportunity emerged, and I was sought out by much more senior professors to help cofound this class with them. I could be the voice of the Black professor and the experienced private equity professional in the classroom at one and the same time.

I haven't shied away from playing this role, even though it shines a light on me culturally. In fact, that's why I was eager to pursue the opportunity: because I culturally had something unique to offer. I leaned into that difference so that I could exercise my superpower and bring it to some important course content.

As I mentioned, the group (in my case, HBS) needs those unique cultural contributions. It benefits from them. Knowing and appreciat-ing your own culture empowers you to contribute to the group. This is not about cultural chauvinism, however—the goal of engaging with your own culture is also to develop an appreciation for the fact that other people come from other cultural backgrounds. This appreciation allows you to build bridges, to communicate across differences. To quote Dr. Metzger one more time, "The higher level of awareness that you have of your own subjectivity, the easier it makes it to liaise and connect with other people … it becomes easier to see when someone else is coming from a different place, and then it makes your communication less garbled." In other words, working on your culture journey is setting yourself up to be a more effective communicator—to be better at being heard and better at hearing.

Following on capability, culture is about getting your own story together and clear to yourself first so that you can then go out and effectively leverage it and communicate it to others. Once you've got that internal story or communication running smoothly, you can then turn to the third of the 5 Cs: communication.

Coaching Tips

- Write out your own cultural balance sheet—feel free to use the template I provide at www.archieljonesjr.com/assessment. It's natural to start with liabilities, but see if you can recast each liability as an asset in the lefthand column, and try to come up with other assets as well so that you can have some equity to balance everything out.

- Think about assets: list three things about your family or household that will help propel you forward on your leadership journey. Consider the successes and failures of previous generations of your family and the lessons you might learn from them.

- Try to memorize the assets column so that you can bring these assets to mind in order to build confidence when you're communicating and making connections. This will help quiet any external negative feedback or internal noise.

- List three cultural heroes with whom you share a background. What do you admire about them? How do you think you might reflect their example in your own leadership journey?

- Learn about your cultural background broadly. How does your culture view the world, human beings, relationships, wealth, and so on? How can you leverage these perspectives to make contributions to your group and to communicate with others more effectively?

CHAPTER 6:

Communication: My Story

*State what you want, and go for it, don't refuse
yourself a request you did not make.*

—BANGAMBIKI HABYARIMANA

Once you've figured out the story you want to tell about yourself, communicating that story to others can be empowering and can take you places you don't expect. In my case, it landed me exactly where I wanted to be, even when I was still unclear on how or if I'd be able to get there.

I didn't think my first job out of college was going to be with Merrill Lynch. Not that I didn't want to go there—it just didn't seem like the natural next step. As an undergrad, I had been in a program called Sponsors for Educational Opportunity (SEO), through which Wall Street recruiters would seek out students from schools that weren't usually represented on Wall Street (including historically Black colleges and universities [HBCUs] like Morehouse). Through that program I ended up as an intern on the trading floor at Salomon Brothers the summer after my junior year, getting my first real exposure to Wall Street and the world of high finance. SEO also exposed me to cocktail hours held by all the various banks, where I was able to meet executives, HR professionals, and other members of the team and start developing relationships.

I had gotten excited about private equity as a junior at Morehouse, and the tried-and-true traditional path, which I expected to follow, involved working for a matter of years in mergers and acquisitions (M&A) before, in a way, graduating to private equity. Basically, you needed to cut your teeth on advising other people on deals and transactions before being able to work on doing your own. Approaching graduation, I was fortunate to receive offers from the two main firms that would put me on that path, the firms doing the largest M&A transactions at the time: Morgan Stanley and Goldman Sachs.

So, I figured I was checking all the right boxes and was all set to be part of a cohort of probably thirty or forty other junior associates in M&A at one of these firms. In the meantime, though, I had also developed a strong relationship with the head of recruitment at Merrill Lynch, who invited me to a Super Saturday event where I would get flown up to New York for a full day of interviews and a steak dinner with some of their bankers. For a college student, that sounded like a pretty cool deal, but at that point I thought I already knew where I was going, so I hesitated. "Just go through and finish out the process," she said. I agreed to, mainly out of respect for her and our relationship (though the steak dinner was also definitely a factor).

After all, what did I have to lose? I had offers in hand from the two biggest M&A firms already, so I might as well meet these M&A folks from Merrill Lynch and see what they had to say. So I flew to New York for the interviews, feeling pretty confident. During one of the interviews, a banker (or at least I assumed he was a banker) named Brad asked me, "So why M&A? We do a lot of things here at Merrill; what interests you about M&A specifically?"

Again feeling like I had no risk involved, nothing to lose, I decided to be bold and somewhat blunt. "I really want to do private equity, and M&A is going to put me on the path to get there," I said. "I honestly don't have much interest in advising other people's transactions; I want to do my own." I told the interviewers about my being inspired by reading about Reginald Lewis, who had passed away not long before. "He's the role model for an exciting type of career that I didn't even know existed before. So going into M&A is really just a kind of two-step to get me where I really want to go."

I was feeling pretty smart and confident at the time, but there was clearly still a lot I didn't know about the banking world. For instance, Brad's name tag identified him as being from "Merrill Lynch Capital Partners," which I didn't realize at the time was language that signaled that he was not in fact a banker but was actually *in* private equity. If I had known I was being interviewed by a private equity partner at the time, I would have been a hell of a lot more nervous and might have played things much closer to the vest. But I didn't know—so I came right out and said, point blank, what I wanted and why I wanted it.

What I also didn't know is that Merrill Lynch had a practice of selecting one or two of each cohort of hundred-some analysts to work in the private equity group—an almost unheard-of opportunity for someone straight out of undergrad, at least at the time. This conversation with Brad got me in the door of having an interview with some of the other private equity folks, who I was then able to tell the same story comfortably and confidently.

I was ultimately selected for the private equity group, and at that time, an idea started to take root in my mind: there was some value in playing my hand aggressively and just asking for what I wanted. In sales, they call it *asking for the order*—just come out and say it.

Now I still didn't always have the confidence to do this, but I started to ask myself the questions that I hope you will start asking yourself in the next couple of chapters: *Why not? Why can't you do it more often? What other opportunities might you have missed because you've held back? What's the worst that could happen if you do it?*

The story I was telling myself at the time—that I had nothing to lose, and that what I really wanted was to go into private equity—led me to change my approach in a way that changed the trajectory of the rest of my life and career. That's why I've focused so much in the last several chapters on the story you tell yourself. It can be life-changing, because it becomes the story you tell others.

GREG WALTON ON TELLING HIS STORY

For Greg, telling his story took confidence at first, but sharing it ultimately became a source of confidence for moving forward on his leadership journey:

> While I was a young adult trying to navigate society and getting a job after going to jail, Year Up utilized me as someone who could go to donor events and share my story and network. And it really helped me build my confidence on connecting with people and having the ability to meet and get to know people from different spaces—black, white, wealth, nonprofit. All of those things were opportunities to help me build my confidence that we're all humans. We all make mistakes. All of that gave me a runway to help build my confidence that I don't have to be defined by my past. We are greater than our mistakes.

I had to build the confidence to get to do that. Because now, and I hear it all the time, people are always like, "Thank you for sharing your story and being transparent and being honest." Actually, I had to get to a place of confidence to be able to feel like I could share that story … Just being open and honest about our mistakes and our journey and everything else is not the easiest thing to do, as I've had to learn. That is a skill, and I had to build the confidence to get to the point where I could do that.

The Other End of the Spectrum

We often spend too much time and effort trying to tell people what we think they want to hear instead of being direct. We shouldn't wait (as I did) until we feel like we have absolutely nothing to lose before we ask for the order. Even where there is some kind of risk involved, rejection, like failure, is rarely fatal.

The flip side of this is not waiting until we're absolutely desperate to ask for help. I've made a version of this mistake too.

After a few years working as a private equity consultant with Parthenon Group, I left to start an entrepreneurial venture, along with a business partner, called Maplegate Holdings. Our goal was to follow a search fund model in order to find a business to buy and operate. Unfortunately, this was just after the dot-com bubble burst, so our timing was bad. In spite of two years of effort and a lot of personal capital invested, a transaction never came to fruition, and Maplegate folded.

As a result, I found myself in a really tough spot. I had exhausted all of my options with Maplegate, and eventually I burned through all the savings I had and started falling behind financially. I did everything I could think of to get myself out of this hole on my own, but eventually my back was against the wall: I had to reach out to my family, my friends, and my network and ask for help.

Why was this so hard? I can think of two main obstacles, which I think apply both in my case and for other people. First, it can be difficult and embarrassing to admit that you don't have it all figured out. In my case: here I was, a Harvard MBA, owned a nice home, had kids in private school—from the outside, I looked like I had things pretty worked out. I didn't though, and I started to fall behind on things, such as paying for that nice home I had. Because of pride and fear of embarrassment, however, I waited until the wolf was nearly at the door before I reached out to ask people for help.

The second obstacle, of course, is fear of rejection. Rejection, when you ask for help, may be the worst-case scenario, but it is far from fatal—especially if you haven't waited until you're desperate to ask for help. By the time I asked for help, I was cooking up horrible scenarios in my mind about what might happen if people told me no.

What actually happened, though, was that people were happy to help. They were especially happy to pay me for my time, availability, and expertise, all of which I had plenty of. This is because one of the ways I asked for help was by *offering* help. For instance, I offered paid consulting services, letting people know I was available and open to work with them on what they were working on. People didn't just help me because I was in a tough spot; a lot of them didn't even know I was struggling at all (which helped on the pride and embarrassment front). I just offered to be available to them, and they took me up on it.

I could have saved myself a lot of pain if I had just broadcast my availability a year earlier. Still, that's how I kickstarted the next phase of my career: going out and asking for help from people I hadn't reached out to before. Again, I found myself thinking, *Why didn't I reach out like this earlier? Why did I wait until my back was against the wall? What's the worst that could have happened if I had just been reaching out to people all along?*

In this case, I was at the opposite end of the spectrum. Instead of having nothing to lose, I felt like I had no other options and a lot to lose. But the core of communication as one of the 5 Cs is learning that you don't need to be at one or the other of these two extremes in order to ask for the order or ask for help. You can communicate your story effectively at any time if you're prepared. The key to effective communication is how you leverage your story to make the ask at the times you're in the middle of the spectrum—which is most of your life, really. Most of the time, there will be some risk involved, but failure will not be a matter of life or death. It's during those times that you have to learn to lean into communication to propel you forward on your leadership journey.

TERRI BRADLEY ON THE BENEFIT OF OFFERING HELP

Terri leverages her superpower of forging positive relationships partly by offering help freely:

> The thing that I always try to do is say, "Is there anything I can do for you?" … I think a lot of start-up founders are always like, "I need, need, need," but they never then say, "Hey, is there anything I can do for you? Are there any relationships that I can connect you with?" And I think people appreciate that …
>
> What is it that I have that I could do for somebody else? … I think you have to put yourself out there and you have to just be very authentic. I think it has helped me really build relationships with folks that I probably would not have had access to just by going into a room, being authentic, being different, I think, than a lot of other founders, and offering to help any way that I can.

Ask Not, Have Not

Everyone, at some point on their leadership journey—especially those who are on an entrepreneurial journey—are going to reach a point like the one I reached after the end of Maplegate. Whatever you're trying to accomplish is going to end up taking longer, costing more, or requiring more effort than you had expected or planned. That's when you have to ask for help. But you don't have to wait until you're desperate to ask for that help. I've seen the same dynamic play out in entrepreneurs who I've coached. They struggle to ask for what they want unless they feel like there is either no risk involved or no other option.

The fact of the matter is, none of us have it all figured out, and we need to get comfortable enough and have the humility to acknowledge that in our day-to-day lives. We all need help! But, as you'll know if you've worked through your capability and culture journeys, we all also have help to offer.

Before I reached out to my network for help in the wake of Maplegate folding, I had not realized how much I was bringing to the table—and this is before I even discovered and started leaning into my superpower of teaching and coaching. I was just offering services on the basis of something I was good at and could help with, which taught me one more important lesson about communication. If you have a story about yourself and what you have to offer worked out, one of the best ways to approach someone to ask for something *you* want is to go to them and offer to help them with something *they* want.

As I tell many of the students and entrepreneurs that I counsel: *You have not because you ask not.* Communicating your story about what you can bring to the table makes asking for help a lot easier to stomach and psych yourself into. You're still putting yourself out there, and there's still some vulnerability and risk involved, but wrapping your ask in a layer of something you have to offer smooths the way a good bit. Having your story ready in your back pocket to share with the world also helps with building the confidence to ask for the order and start moving forward on your leadership journey. When I finally did discover my superpower, I just started referring to myself as a coach, telling other people that that's what I did, and that opened doors to new opportunities for me.

So the story you tell yourself about yourself is still very important when it comes to communication, because it becomes the story you tell others. This is the core of communication as the third C: telling the world about your superpower, your unique cultural contribution, and where you want to go on your leadership journey. Communicating these things will allow you to position yourself for what you want to achieve, whether that is joining someone else's or some organization's journey or recruiting others to join yours. The next chapter digs into some techniques and strategies for developing skills in this area.

Prompts for Reflection

- Think of your superpower and the hidden cultural gems you've uncovered in your journey through the first two Cs. Practice telling yourself a story about yourself that highlights these assets.

- Consider how to uncover that hidden voice and share it so that you're communicating that same story of what you have to offer to others.

CHAPTER 7:

Communication: Your Story

Sometimes all you have to do is ask and it leads to all your dreams coming true. Ask those questions. Just ask them. More often than you'd suspect, the answer you get is, "Sure."

—RANDY PAUSCH

One day, a week or so after students had returned from the holiday break for the spring semester, Benedita dropped by my office.

"I just wanted to say thanks for helping me get through that first semester. I really learned a lot," she said.

"Happy to help," I replied. We proceeded to talk about the confidence she had developed in Finance I (as well as in her other courses) and how that confidence would help her in the courses she was taking her second semester.

"You've racked up some good wins with your grades last semester. I was really happy to hear from you a lot more in class toward the end of the semester, and I know your other professors were too," I said.

"I was able to get more and more excited about bringing a creative, puzzle-solving approach to the course material, so that helped a lot, and I started to feel more like I had a unique perspective to offer, instead of feeling like I didn't belong or wasn't welcome," she acknowledged.

"So, what comes next? Have you thought about what you'll be doing this summer?" I asked. An important part of the second semester for HBS students involves figuring out their summer plans, which usually involve lining up an internship, a job, or some other type of project that will help propel them forward toward what they want to do after business school.

"I guess I'll just be going back to BCG to work for the summer," she said.

"Well, I seem to remember you saying you ultimately wanted to do something a little more ambitious. Why not get started on that? You stretched and got outside your comfort zone a good bit last semester; let's keep that up. How do you think you could stretch for the summer?" The summer between the two years of business school tends to be a stretch of time where students can try something new without too much being at stake, so I often recommend that they experiment and take some calculated risks. Whatever they do, they'll still likely be able to leverage it into a full-time job by the time they're in their second year. "If you could get away with whatever you dream up, what would you do?"

She thought for a second. "Well, for one thing, I'd really love to go back to Brazil for as long as possible," she said. "I don't know; I haven't had much opportunity to think about this social enterprise idea, which is what I'd really like to do. It would be great if I could somehow get to work on that, but I'm not even sure what that would entail."

"Gosh, if only you knew some people who could help you with that," I said, smiling.

She laughed. "OK, you're right; what better place than HBS to figure this out? I just don't even know where to begin."

"You just need to figure out who can help you and ask them for help. Just like you did when you first came to my office hours. I'm thrilled that you feel safe and comfortable coming to me for help, but how are you going to approach people you don't already have a connection with for help?"

"Like who?" she asked.

"Other professors, to start with," I said. "There are folks teaching here with experience and expertise in the social enterprise world. If you reach out to them and tell them what you're passionate about and want to do, I'm sure some of them would be happy to spend some time helping you. Also, some of your fellow students could be valuable resources, especially if they share your mission. Did you know there's a social enterprise club?"

"Yeah, I remember seeing something about that."

"What better way to get started on your planning than joining that and drawing on the collective resources of classmates who share your passion for making a social impact?" I said. "With your classmates and with professors, and even with other folks in the HBS alumni network, telling your story and presenting what you have to offer is going to be your best tool for effectively getting other people to invest in you."

The result of her capability and culture journeys already had Benedita telling a new story about herself. Her communication journey would involve her starting to share that story with others to propel her farther along on her leadership journey.

Reframing the Ask

Often, when we want to communicate, it's because we want something from someone. Whether we're applying for a job, ordering dinner, or simply hoping a friend or acquaintance will acknowledge us and listen to us, we are typically asking for *something*. Obstacles to communication tend to arise, then, because asking for something always comes along with the fear of rejection. If we let fear of rejection take over, we shut down the possibility of communicating.

On top of that, with asking for help in particular (as I mentioned in the previous chapter), we can add pride and the fear of embarrassment to our list of obstacles. Asking for help can seem like a display of weakness.

Part of what is empowering about discovering your superpower and your cultural assets, though, is that you can now practice approaching communication, even when asking for help, from a more confident standpoint. Instead of "Woe is me; can you help me out?" the conversation can begin with, "Here's what I'm great at and what I have to offer. How can I help you?" This puts you on the giving end rather than the receiving, which is empowering. Now you're at least on an equal footing with the person you're approaching, so some sort of back-and-forth, an exchange, can occur.

Approaching communication this way, at least to some degree and in certain contexts, is necessary for moving forward and getting things done on your leadership journey. This is why I counsel all my students to take some coursework on negotiation in their second year. Whether they're going to be a start-up founder, a manager of a team, a salesperson, or whatever, those negotiation skills will be the key to enhancing their effectiveness.

The first step, though, is digging into the capability and culture journeys. Once you've done that, and once you've calibrated the story you're telling yourself with what's going to move you forward on your leadership journey, you've also started to build up a supply of talking points that will be what you present to other people. Once you know what you're best at or what unique treasure you have to offer, you know what you're going to be telling people about. And again, you'll often be telling them about it in the context of asking how you can leverage it to help them. So the first step to effective communication is asking yourself: *What can I offer? How can I leverage my superpower and cultural assets to benefit other people?*

As we discussed in the chapters on culture, the goal is not to assimilate or bill yourself as having the same skills and assets as everyone else. As any good marketer will tell you, the goal is *differentiation*. If you're selling a product and you want people to pick that product over a competing product, you have to show how your product stands out. If you're charging twice as much, you have to show why your product brings *at least* twice as much value as the competitor's, and the only way to do this is by differentiating—drawing attention to the unique assets and value-adding features of your product.

The same goes for when you're trying to get others to invest their time or money in your personal leadership journey. If you're a generalist rather than a specialist—if you're trying to be all things to whoever may come along—you're just going to blend into the crowd, fade into the background, and be unable to leverage your assets. If all you want to do is make the team, you may be willing to play any position—but you aren't going to offer much value in any of those positions. To maximize your impact, the value of your contribution, and your potential for success, you ultimately have to specialize.

This can be scary. Narrowing your specialized focus to be aligned with your capability and culture is going to close off certain opportunities to you. To build leadership capital, though, you need to give people a reason to invest *their* capital in *you*. If you're asking for something—help, guidance, mentorship, collaboration, or whatever—you have to start with what you have to give in return. Not only does this increase your likelihood of success, but it also helps to reframe the situation so that overcoming the obstacles to communication, such as pride or fear of rejection, becomes much easier.

TERRI BRADLEY ON THE CHALLENGE
OF ASKING FOR HELP

Terri acknowledges her own struggles with asking for help but maintains that finding a way to do so is crucial for success:

> I'll be stuck, stuck, stuck. And I'm up all night instead of saying, *Hey, you built this amazing network of really smart people. Ask for help.*
>
> You feel this tremendous pressure to win, because there's so many people betting on you and wanting to see you be successful … But then you're like, *OK, but if things aren't going great, how do I say that to all these people who have bet on me, or who have invested in me, their time, talent, treasure?*
>
> … So just trying to figure out how transparent you can be with those folks—when you talk about communication, I think that's a big part of it. I think that has been the best thing that I've done: create that community where I can be vulnerable and I can say, *Things are really great and I'm really super excited*, or I can say *Things are not-so-great* or *Here's this big challenge that I'm having* and not feel as though I'll be judged.

Rewriting Your Bio

What we're really talking about with figuring out how you're going to communicate what you uniquely offer, from a capability and culture perspective, is your *personal brand*. Your personal brand is the outward display of the story you're telling yourself after going through the capability and culture journeys. If you've grappled with these journeys, you should be able to tell your story authentically instead of dumbing it down or tailoring it to what you think your audience wants to hear.

For instance, one of the first things I did after grappling with my superpower and determining that I wanted to go in the direction of coaching and teaching was restructure my résumé and rewrite my personal bio. I didn't need to label myself a CFO anymore; my résumé needed to say *coach* on it. And the bio that appeared, for instance, on my LinkedIn profile needed to tell a story about myself as a coach and a teacher, not just as a finance professional.

Benedita and I worked on retailoring her personal brand and leveraging it in communication with her classmates and professors. Instead of being "the Brazilian woman who works for BCG," she needed to start describing herself as a budding entrepreneur who wanted to have some social impact in the area of education. Even after coming back in the spring after a strong first semester, she still wasn't quite ready to describe herself this way—it was like a secret she was afraid or embarrassed to speak out loud. I encouraged her that, if she was going to make progress on this goal, she had to overcome the fear and proclaim her brand publicly.

To help her with this, I walked her through an exercise I've gone through with a lot of students and entrepreneurs I've mentored. "You need to write up two new biography blurbs. The one you have on your HBS student profile now is strong, but it focuses almost entirely on your schools and your work at BCG—the name brands you're associated with. Leave that stuff for your résumé. We need to round out your bios so they communicate your *personal* brand."

"Why a couple? If I have one authentic personal brand, shouldn't I just have one bio?" she asked.

"Well, the first round isn't the one you're going to be putting on LinkedIn or sending out to potential employers, or even the elevator speech you're going to give when you're networking. You're not going to show it to anybody—you don't even have to show it to me if you don't want to. As long as you write it out for yourself, it should help.

"I don't want any modesty or self-consciousness to get in the way," I told her, "because what you're going to do is write a bio where you brag as much as possible about all of your accomplishments and your assets, including your superpower and cultural assets. Speak firmly, and don't downplay anything. Don't make it fictional of course—just state the facts in the best possible light. The fact of the matter is you don't *need* to make stuff up. Yeah, you may feel a little silly while you're doing it and laugh at yourself a little bit. That's fine. And even if you crumple it up and throw it away when you're done, or delete the document, or whatever your method is—just give it one readthrough before you do, and you'll realize that you're more badass than you give yourself credit for and put yourself out there as. You will shift the lens you look at yourself through to some degree."

She was skeptical, but she agreed to give it a try. "And what's the second thing I'm going to write?" she asked.

"That's the official version," I explained, "the actual bio that you put on your profile and share with the world, the story you tell people when you introduce yourself to them. We'll worry about that down the line, though—trust me, after you write out this first version, that second one is going to look a hell of a lot different."

Anyone can do this exercise, of course. After uncovering your superpower and your cultural assets, this is a good way to start developing your internal story into one that you can communicate to the world. Even though you may never show your "brag" bio to anyone, the next time you're called upon to write a personal statement, for instance, or draft a blurb for your LinkedIn profile, you'll be much more likely to construct it in a way that authentically tells your story and isn't bashful about your accomplishments or your aspirations. This can build confidence, and it can also make you more effective when you're ready to go out on a limb and ask for what you really want.

Asking for the Order

The final step of the communication journey is confidently stepping out and proclaiming what you want to the people who can give it to you, or at least help you to attain or achieve it. We call this *asking for the order*. In asking for the order, you want to ask for something above and beyond—a stretch goal that's an order of magnitude above what you think you can safely get.

We tend to ask for less than what we really want, because we tend to ask for what we think we are likely to get—there's that fear of rejection at work again. Coming out of undergrad, for instance, I didn't even try to pursue a private equity position, because going into M&A first was the expected route. I only spoke what I really wanted aloud after I had ensured the safety of having what I thought I could get.

I could have gone the same route when it came to teaching. What I really wanted was to go back to HBS to teach, but I could have pursued other teaching work to ramp myself up to that. I could have started by pursuing the high probability options. There are several colleges and universities in Georgia, including my alma mater, and many of them would welcome a successful local businessperson with a Harvard MBA to come and lecture there. Perhaps it would have been safer to start there and work my way up to being ready to teach at HBS.

But why not at least ask for what I really wanted? Why do we pursue opportunities in our lives any differently than how we think about applying to colleges? For many people, the smart route to go is to have a safety school you know you can attend, some high probability schools, and then at least one reach school—the dream school where you'd really love to go, even though it may be a bit above and beyond. There is some risk of rejection, but you've got the safety and other high probability schools there in your back pocket to mitigate that risk. You still apply to the reach school, don't you?

Why not approach asking for the order in this same way? Maybe you line up some higher probability opportunities to offset your loss in case of rejection but still make the case for why you deserve something that might seem a bit ambitious. This is how you start to compress the time it takes to move through the steps to get what you want faster.

Again, just look at my experience with HBS. My timeline for teaching there, which I had aspired to do for quite some time, had me pursuing it after my kids had all gone to college and I was relatively on my own and ready. That would make it, say, 2024. Once I decided to lean into my superpower, though, I thought I might be able to compress the timeline if I got a *Yes*—and that is exactly what happened. I jumped ahead in my plans by nearly five years.

Even if the answer had been *No*, I wouldn't have really lost anything. Worst-case scenario, they shut the door in my face, and I have to figure out what to do next. That can sting, but it won't kill you. Rejection is never fatal.

Even more likely, though, is that the door won't be *completely* shut in your face; rather, there will be room for a follow-up conversation that will help you more fully understand the path you need to take to get what you want. If HBS had turned me away, I wouldn't have had to go home and give up forever on teaching. I would have had a decision to make about what to do next—the ball would be back in my court, and I would have the power to figure out the next step. You are rarely stuck in a binary *Yes, you can/No, you can't* situation. Even if the answer is *No*, it means *Not right now*, and then your job is to find out *when* and *how*.

So, all I risked was being left where I was before—with a five-year plan and some intermediate steps to take. In fact, the *No* answer can actually help you make progress itself, because that follow-up conversation makes the path all that much clearer. This is a better place to be than chasing some set of mystery criteria. Even if you're asking for something that seems to be an order of magnitude beyond what you think you can safely attain, the risk of asking is low, and the potential reward—*What if you get it?*—considerably higher.

Do whatever you can to build your confidence for yourself and to make that case to whoever you're asking for the order from. In my case, I reviewed the entire curriculum of courses taught at HBS and was able to identify a couple dozen for which I could tell myself, *Sure, I could jump in and teach that today*. Telling myself that story made it easier to present my case to the folks at HBS when I was ready.

We'll talk about connection in later chapters, but it also helped that I was hooked into a network around HBS that helped me prepare and gain access. I was an alum, of course, but I had also spent time on campus in the intervening years working on venture competitions and coordinating activities among the alumni network. This means I had put myself, my superpower, and my passion on display in a way that was visible to the decision makers at HBS.

To ask for an order that's above and beyond, it helps to have a record of performance like this, both for the sake of your own confidence and for the sake of making your case. Ideally, the people you're asking should have already seen you in action delivering results above and beyond what's expected. By demonstrating your capability, you're giving them a reason to want to invest in you, and your ask isn't coming out of the blue.

When I worked at Parthenon Group right after business school, I was taking work off my supervisor Samantha's plate in addition to doing my own work. I didn't ask for any recognition for doing that. What I ultimately attained, though, was Samantha's sponsorship. When it came time for me to potentially lead my own transaction, Samantha was there to back me up and say that I was capable, because I had already been delivering results for her. Showing your superpower and delivering results earn you the right to ask for the order.

Benedita learned the same lesson. A month or so into the spring semester, we had positioned her to make a bit of a bold ask of her employer, BCG. She had shifted her internal story, of course, and she had recast her bio and elevator speech to reflect that story more boldly. Crucially, though, at the same time, she had already been demonstrating her value to BCG through her work both there and at HBS. When she could point to her work successes as instances of leveraging her superpower of creative puzzle-solving, she could more convincingly make the case for herself in asking for something more.

"I'm not ready to jump completely into the deep end," Benedita told me. "I still think I should do something within BCG—*but*," she went on, excited, "I realized that BCG actually has offices in São Paulo, and I could request to be transferred there!"

"That's terrific!" I said. "Will this help you make progress on your social enterprise idea?"

"Mmm, not so much, I guess. I've asked for help and advice from some of the other professors and students here about what it takes to get something like that going, and I've learned a lot from them. I do have some ideas—but I think that would require working outside BCG, and that feels like too big a risk at this point."

"Fair enough," I said. "Have you considered splitting your summer up? You've got twelve weeks between semesters to play with. You could spend six with BCG, hopefully in Brazil, and then devote the other six weeks to your own project, whatever that looks like."

Her eyes widened. "I didn't even realize I could do that!"

"Look," I said, "you're in good with BCG. You've earned the right to ask for the order. Worst-case scenario, they say no. But maybe you could at least get back to Brazil for the summer, even if you're with BCG the whole time. It doesn't hurt to ask."

She took a deep breath. "OK," she said. "I think I can do this."

Benedita told her story and made her case to her supervisors at BCG, and she was able to get exactly what she wanted: she would be paired with a consulting team in São Paulo for the first six weeks of the summer, after which she would have the rest of the summer off to work on her own project. Her next task would be to figure out what that looked like: would she team up with some other social entrepreneur, try to find a position in an existing organization, or set out on her own trying to finance a start-up?

Benedita had tackled all the key aspects of communication: asking for help (from me, other professors, and her classmates); telling her story (by communicating her superpower, the unique value she had to offer, and her passion); and ultimately asking for the order from BCG. Doing the first two steps so effectively helped build up her confidence for the third and ended up ensuring her success in getting what she wanted. For her summer project to be a success, though, she would need to flex her communication muscles more fully and start leveraging her network.

Coaching Tips

- Try the biography writing exercise I went through with Benedita. Don't worry about what you write being published or read by anyone. Write boldly rather than tamping down any of your assets, accomplishments, and aspirations. This can be a first step to more confidently and authentically telling your story.

- Whatever your goal, reverse engineer the shortest and most effective path to accomplishing it. For each step along the way, determine who can help you with it and reach out to that person.

- List five people whom you admire, share a mission with, and who could help you on your leadership journey. Do the research to figure out how to get in touch with them. If they seem too distant to reach out to directly, find another person who may be connected to them that you can access and reach out to that person. If you come up empty, just list five more people, rinse, and repeat. You've lost nothing but a little time. This exercise is a safe way to start tiptoeing into the next of the 5 Cs: connection.

CHAPTER 8:

Connection: My Story

How can you grow tired of helping others
when by doing so you help yourself?

—MARCUS AURELIUS

I haven't *applied* for a job, in the traditional sense that most people are familiar with, in over two decades. Sure, I've put myself out there, made myself available, and worked hard to get where I am, but I haven't submitted a formal application, to be reviewed by a hiring committee made up of people who don't know anything else about me, in more than twenty years.

Instead, my opportunities have come to me because I've been telling my story and leveraging my unique offerings, my superpower and my cultural background. That communication by itself, though, wasn't enough—I also had to communicate these things within the context of a *network* of people I had cultivated relationships with over the years. This type of *connection* can be an extraordinarily powerful catalyst to move you forward toward whatever treasure you seek.

Much of connection involves planting seeds, even though you might not know when and how they will bear fruit. Take, for instance, the story of how I got my first position on the board of directors of a public company. Now, I had reached a place in my career where I was feeling comfortable and confident; I had been serving on the boards of some nonprofits and social enterprises, and I was ready to take the next step. I wanted to serve on the board of a public company, and I would share this ambition with anybody who would listen. I communicated it assertively, and I was taking all the right traditional steps: joining the right organizations and getting the right certifications to make myself an attractive candidate. The opportunity, though, came from an unexpected place: someone I hadn't even spoken to in a few years.

Back in the '90s, before I went to business school, I did some consulting work at Parthenon as an intern and established a relationship with a man there named John Coughlin, who taught me a lot about the consulting world. Several years down the line, I was able to invest in John just as he had invested in me early on: he decided to transition out of consulting and into M&A, and he sought out my advice. I provided him with some counsel on possible roles in M&A and private equity and how to think about that kind of work—in retrospect, I realize that I was providing him with some coaching, deploying my superpower in a small way.

He went on to a few different roles in that world, and we continued our relationship more as friends than in any professional capacity—just casually staying in touch, seeing each other now and then because our sons go to school together. I hadn't spoken to him directly in a few years when, one evening, he called and left me a voicemail: "Arch, I'd love to catch up when you have a minute. Give me a call."

I didn't think much of it—if anything I thought maybe it had to do with something going on with our sons at high school. I was busy with my day-to-day work at the time, so it took a few days for me to get back to him, and we actually ended up playing some phone tag. If he needed something from me, it didn't seem terribly urgent, so I was a bit stunned when I finally got on the phone with him and the real subject matter of the call came to light: "Archie, do you have any interest in being on a public company board?"

As I mentioned, I had been working this goal, but I had not discussed it with John, so I was a bit dumbfounded, but I quickly said, "I sure am. What do you have in mind?"

"Well, as you may know," he said, "I'm now serving as a senior executive at FLEETCOR, running M&A for them, and reporting directly to the CEO, Ron Clarke. Ron recently came to the leadership team and told us he'd love to bring someone new onto the board of directors, and if there was anyone we thought particularly highly of, to let him know. So now I'm just calling to see if you're interested."

Within a week, I had an interview with the CEO of FLEETCOR. A few weeks later I had been vetted and interviewed by the rest of the board, and I was en route to being elected to the board at its next meeting. With that, I had achieved a major goal I had been pursuing, all because I took a call from an old buddy. Our relationship dated back to 1997. I had continued to invest in that relationship both personally and professionally but with no real thought about what I might get out of it in terms of real gain. Out of the blue, though, it turned into my first public board assignment in 2020.

Leveraging connection on your leadership capital journey involves sowing with your superpower and your effort, investing in others, not in a transactional way, but still in a way that you will be able to reap rewards from later on. It has a lot in common with what we call *karma* from a spiritual perspective. From a more business-minded perspective, you can view it as superpower R&D, marketing, and development. If you invest in connection, it pays off in different ways down the line. Even the opportunity to leverage, develop, and hone your superpower, which you can do by investing in others, is in a sense its own reward.

Sow Now, Reap Later

When I gave John advice early in his M&A career, I had no thought that this would lead to a board assignment, or to anything at all, for that matter. I just saw John as a worthwhile guy to invest some of my time and effort in. I liked him and wanted to be helpful. This still counts as leveraging connection. We often think of *networking* as approaching relationships in a transactional way: *You scratch my back and I'll scratch yours*. But this is a mistake. Connection, as one of the 5 Cs, involves recognizing that leveraging a network doesn't work this way. Like any investment, you have to start by putting some capital into a relationship before you can think about drawing from it. Effectively leveraging a network involves sowing now without thought to what you will reap. In fact, there can be quite a bit of distance between your sowing and your reaping, as my relationship with John shows.

These unexpected benefits have been characteristic of my own journey over the past few decades. You may recall that I got my first position in private equity straight out of undergrad, all because I agreed to finish out the recruiting process by attending that Super Saturday event as a favor for the recruiter whom I'd previously developed a relationship with. There was no *quid pro quo* involved, but my investment in the relationship bore fruit nonetheless.

More often, relationships bear fruit much further down the line. Relationship capital, which we mentioned in chapter 1, plays its most prominent role here in talking about connection. Like a lot of investments, you have to let capital accumulate over time before you can benefit from the payout. This was true of my relationship with John and also of my journey of leadership in the social sector.

Toward the end of my first year as a student at HBS, I did a volunteer consulting project with two social entrepreneurs. I helped them develop a business plan based on their idea for how to get nonprofit organizations to scale effectively. Again, I didn't see myself as a coach at the time and didn't think about it in terms of leveraging my superpower, but that's essentially what I was doing. I had acquired some skills in the private equity field, and I coached them in the tools, techniques, and frameworks of that world to assist them in their mission to reinvent how the social sector operates.

I worked on this project over the course of a year with a team of other volunteers, with no expectation of gaining anything from it other than experience and an opportunity to exercise my own skills and learn some new ones, which was rewarding in itself. In the years following, New Profit, the organization these entrepreneurs founded on the basis of the business plan I helped develop, went on to become a pioneering force in the emerging world of impact investing. Meanwhile, when my attempts to make Maplegate viable were winding down and I was reaching out to my network for help, I had the opportunity to go to work at New Profit as a partner, where I worked on some really great projects.

Fast-forward to now, and one of the founders has left New Profit to found Project Evident, which I chair the board of. I also continue to work in partnership with New Profit through the Social Enterprise Initiative at HBS. So my social sector journey continues today, all thanks to my investing my time and my superpower in these social entrepreneurs back when I was a business student.

My relationship with Rudy Karsan, which I discussed in chapter 1, is another example of investing in a relationship paying dividends far down the line. I spent a lot of time coaching Rudy on his transaction in late 1999, ultimately ending up on the board for his company. I left that board position a couple of years later to devote my time to Maplegate. By the time 2005 rolled around, I was done with Maplegate, helping out at New Profit, and looking for more opportunities, when I got a call from Rudy telling me that his company, Kenexa, was about to go public.

First, he just wanted to give me the opportunity to buy some shares at Kenexa's initial public offering (IPO), which I did. At the same time, I was still feeling the pinch financially. I had left a great private equity gig to try something entrepreneurial that didn't have the success I had hoped for, and I was slowly figuring out my way back to a comfortable position by helping out in the impact investing arena. I still wasn't sure what came next for me, though.

Kenexa specializes in human capital management, which at the time was a relatively young space where a lot of small companies were operating. Rudy's strategy with going public, which I had helped him develop several years before, was going to be to try to consolidate that space and build a global set of capabilities. About a month after the IPO, Rudy called me again.

"Hey, Archie," he said, "to execute on this strategy, we're going to have to embark on a pretty ambitious program of mergers and acquisitions. And I need somebody who knows the finance side of M&A to come run that program for us. How about it?"

Rudy didn't know it, but he was offering me a lifeline. I instantly went from running a failing company to helping build a very successful one. I ran global M&A for Kenexa from 2005 to 2012. But again, the seeds for that success had been planted years before as a junior finance professional coaching a business owner on his transaction, with no expectation that anything more would come of his success for me personally.

In all of these cases, I was looking for opportunities, and I was ready when they came my way, but in none of these cases did I make a specific ask of any of the people involved. By exercising my superpower to help other people, to invest in them, I was building relationship capital that would pay off for me down the line.

GREG WALTON ON THE POWER OF CONNECTION

Greg tells a powerful story of how a relationship he developed as a young man re-entered his life at a crucial moment, to his benefit:

> An example of one immediate connection that always rings true and that I immediately think about is a high school guidance counselor who I met as a freshman, who pretty much was my go-to person for all things in high school for the four years that I was there. And they would uniquely end up becoming in that journey what I would call my guardian angel. At some of my lowest moments of my journey—of winding up in jail after college and trying to figure out what to do with my life—they began to be a beacon for me to, one, help build my confidence that I just made a mistake and I wasn't going to be defined by that mistake, but two, show the value of the connection they had with me as a teenager through early adulthood.
>
> And that connection meant something to them, and they valued that and wanted to invest into me in a powerful way, and reached out via letter as a communication to stay

connected. It really was the catalyst to get me connected with other like-minded people. They connected me with Year Up—they connected me with someone there in admissions who had a similar connection to them and partnered us together. But I think about that as an immediate person who, man, had I not made such a strong connection with them in high school, I don't think the outcome of that happens at all.

Investing in Relationships

Investing relationship capital involves putting your superpower to work to help others on their journeys, and you can reap the rewards of that investment by enlisting those others to help you on your journey, in turn. Investing in others by way of your superpower builds your relationship capital account.

Whatever treasure you seek, whatever goal you're trying to achieve, you can't attain it totally on your own. This is why asking for help was such an important message of the communication journey, and the connection journey deepens that message with an important lesson: when you're looking for a way to move forward, *the answer is in your network*.

This may be discouraging to some people, who see themselves as introverts or as not-so-great at networking. We all know that one person or couple of people who just seem like rock stars at getting to know people, keeping in touch with them, and having connections with seemingly everyone. And maybe you're a little jealous of that person, because you know that you just don't have that in you—it isn't part of your personality. I have good news: you don't have to be that person in order to effectively take advantage of connection as part of your leadership journey.

I'm certainly not that rock star. As for how *good* I am at networking, I'd give myself a solid C-plus—maybe a B-minus. Now, I'm a pretty tough grader, but still, I know I'm no rock star, and even so every opportunity I've had in the past twenty years has come from someone in my network. I've been able to reap an extraordinary amount of value from connection even as a fairly average player of the networking game.

I'm not the schmoozing type, but I get along with people, and I invest in my relationships with them. How do you invest in relationships? Help other people along on their own journeys. Just as we saw with communication, offering help and delivering value are going to be foundational to successfully leveraging connection. Even my position teaching at HBS came about this way. I was a known quantity to the people I asked for the order from at Harvard, because I had spent years coaching and mentoring their students, doing venture competitions, and leading reunion and fundraising events through the alumni network. I just stayed in touch with people and tried to be as helpful as possible, without thinking of what I might get out of it other than gratification. But still, when I did end up going to make the ask for a teaching position, I had set myself up as someone they were willing to invest in, because they saw that I was already invested in the school and its students.

So really, almost everything I've done in my career has come to me on some level through prior relationships that I had invested in and that then came full circle in the form of someone being willing to invest in me. That's the power of connection.

With the help of others in your network, you can lighten your load and cover more ground on your leadership journey with less effort. As you develop your network, you'll find that you have connected with people who are in key positions along the critical path to the treasure you seek. In the next chapter, we'll talk about ways to leverage those connections to get you further along on that critical path.

TERRI BRADLEY ON NETWORKING

Like many of us, Terri finds networking difficult and intimidating, too. "Nobody believes me, but I'm really an introvert," she says. She provides some practical, brass-tacks advice for trying to connect with people via online networks like LinkedIn:

> Make sure your profile is up to date and that you're posting, because when you try to connect with people, they're going to look and see what you've got going on. So if you're only connecting with people, but you don't have anything in your profile, you haven't put any thought leadership out, or you haven't put anything about your business, then they're going to look at that and wonder, "What are they about?"
>
> When you then reach out to people, don't just send a connection request. Put something in your connection request: "Hi, I'm so-and-so, this is what I'm doing. I saw your stuff and it sounds interesting…" And actually do look at their stuff—I think that's very important. You have to do that research instead of just mass connecting with people, so you make authentic connection requests…
>
> But make sure your stuff is tight first and that you're putting stuff out there, so when they go to check to verify that you are who you say you are and you're doing what you say you're doing, your profile reflects that.

Prompts for Reflection

- What does networking mean to you?

- What emotional reaction do you have to the idea of networking? If you have a negative reaction, is that holding you back from building stronger connections or leveraging the connections you have?

- What grade would you give yourself as a networker? How can you improve that grade?

- Start thinking about who is in your network already. Who is not in your network that you would like to be?

CHAPTER 9:

Connection: Your Story

A man's growth is seen in the successive choirs of his friends.

—RALPH WALDO EMERSON

The next time I saw Benedita, I expected her to be excited about getting permission from her employers at BCG to split her summer into two six-week chunks so that she could spend time on her own project. Instead, she seemed panicked.

"I'm like the dog chasing the car," she said. "I got what I asked for, and now I don't know what the heck I'm going to do with it!"

I had her share some of what she had learned so far that semester from reaching out to others.

"The professors I've talked to have been really helpful, but what I've been most excited about is the social enterprise club. Some of the students in there are trying to do such interesting stuff, and I've told them that I'm interested in helping and have a puzzle-solving superpower, so people are starting to ask me to help on projects. I'm helping them organize a social entrepreneurship conference here on campus. I also finally got around to doing my My Take, which I got some really exciting feedback on."

During the course of their first year—typically in the first semester, but sometimes in the second—HBS students give a talk called *My Take*, where they introduce themselves, tell a little bit (or sometimes a lot!) of their own story, and share what they're interested in or passionate about. Benedita had put hers off until the second semester because she was feeling very unsure about it. Fortunately, by the time her turn came around, she was feeling much more confident in her own story and was able to effectively communicate that story to the other students in her cohort.

"It has led to making some exciting connections with other people. I'd gone out for drinks with a couple of people here and there, but now this semester I'm starting to really connect with people with a purpose. I'm realizing I'd been sitting in a room with people the whole first semester who were passionate about some of the same things as me, and I had no idea."

Benedita was finding that she had a hidden community she had not been tapping into as close to her as the ninety students in her section. An incoming MBA class at HBS is around a thousand people, and that group is divided into sections of just under a hundred people each who actually end up being in the core classes together. Each section is arranged to optimize diversity—in Benedita's section, for instance, there were students from twenty-three different countries. Students end up making close and valuable connections within their section because of being in classes together and presenting their My Take talks to one another. The connections they make in that group, which is a community we can describe as being part of their second ring (the people they're directly in contact with), in turn, connect them to a wide variety of third-ring people and organizations.

"I've been talking a lot with Frank," she continued, "who had volunteered with an education-based nonprofit back in his hometown in Colorado, and he's seen a lot of what goes into the operations of that type of organization, so he's giving me some ideas on what to do—and what *not* to do. I'm really thinking I might be able to get involved in something this summer that will have some real impact back home. I've also met a couple of students who've worked on social enterprises in developing countries, so I'm going to talk to them more and see what I can learn from them."

The surprising connections Benedita was making—both connections with people and connections among ideas for how to have positive impact in her community—exemplify the rewards that begin to accumulate at this point in the leadership journey. These are the rewards of a fully leveraged network.

"Keep in mind that a big part of the value you're taking away from your Harvard MBA is going to be the network of HBS alums," I told her. "That's tens of thousands of leaders in business and government around the world. You've connected with your classmates, but now you're also ready to start leveraging that larger network." I reminded her of the three rings—starting with herself and then moving out to the second ring of people she was in direct contact with. "Connection really starts to work its magic when you start reaching out and bringing third-ring people into your second ring. And now that you know what your treasure is, you can start leveraging that network to move you further along the critical path to attaining it."

Networking with a Purpose

The key message of the connection journey, which Benedita had arrived at and is the next step after you've started communicating your story to others, is this: *The answer is in your network*. Success is driven by relationships. Whatever treasure you seek, finally attaining it will be the result, not only of your own work but also of the relationships you have cultivated over time. That is why it is so important to make connections and to invest in the relationships that result. In forging those connections and cultivating those relationships, it's crucial to start with giving, to offer your superpower as an investment in the missions of others, with the understanding that you will be on the receiving end of others investing in you further down the line.

Benedita was making purposeful connections within her second ring, her network, and offering to help—sowing seeds. She hadn't thought about it up until that point, but her second ring also included people she knew back in Brazil, some of whom might have local connections that could further help her on her journey. If she was continuing to cultivate those relationships and invest in those people, she could expect that to pay off in time.

Reaching out into the third ring is not only a different skill set but also an essential part of the connection journey, especially if your treasure lies in having third-ring impact. As you invest in connecting outside of your immediate network, you sow seeds that will sprout across a larger area, so to speak. Then, when the time to reap the benefit comes, you will receive investments in *your* journey from people not just in your immediate network but also from outside it. It may not even be the same folks you connected with and invested in in the first place. As you are out sharing your superpower in a way that gives it broader impact, you'll build your reputation and become a person who people are willing to give a positive reference or referral to, or to invest in directly.

As we saw in my own connection journey, relationships that you invest in can pay off in unexpected ways. That doesn't mean, however, that you can't be strategic about who you try to develop connections with. This is where the nuts and bolts of that old term *networking* come in. Some people shudder when they hear the word; it conjures up images of awkward cocktail parties where everyone is a stranger. And there are certainly better and worse ways to go about building a network. There are a handful of ways that the connection journey can go wrong.

One of the most common networking mistakes people make can already be avoided if you've gone through the communication portion of the 5 Cs—namely, trying to network without a purpose. If you haven't figured out what superpower and cultural value you have to offer, then you won't be communicating as effectively, and you may be trying to network as if you're just trying to gather names in a list of conversations you've had. This may also happen if you don't have some conception of the treasure you're seeking and are just networking for the sake of networking.

There are certainly those who network this way—they may even be the type of person you think of when you think of a "good networker." Let's call this type *Surface-level Sarah*. Surface-level Sarah seems to know everyone; her list of contacts is miles long. But that's because she approaches networking more like a sport, where she's just trying to build a list of names rather than making connections with people in order to invest in them or get them to invest in her for some larger purpose. Her range may be broad, but her relationships lack the depth required for those connections to really work their magic. Will anyone on her list really stick their neck out and be a sponsor for her?

Again, if you've read this far, it shouldn't be too much of a challenge to avoid being this person. If you're at the connection stage of the leadership journey, you'll be able to start making *purposeful* connections that lead to a mutually beneficial exchange, just as Benedita started doing when she started speaking to students in her section and in the social enterprise club.

It's important to remember, though, that the way to establish those connections is not to go to people and ask how they can help *you* but to put your superpower on display and ask how you can help *them*. You have to give in order to put yourself in a position to receive. We can call the networker who misses this point *Oscar the Opportunist*. You may know someone like this. When you get a phone call from Oscar the Opportunist, you just know he's going to be asking you for something—money, a favor, a reference, whatever. But when you need one of those things, you know Oscar the Opportunist is not going to be around. The give-and-receive of meaningful connection only works one way here, which actually hurts Oscar because it means that people are going to stop being willing to invest in him, because they know he doesn't invest in others in return.

Don't be Oscar the Opportunist. Start with giving, with offering help, before you think about receiving. Also remember, as I made clear in the previous chapter, that even if you start with giving, there still may be a substantial amount of time before that receiving rolls around. Our last type, whom we'll call *Transactional Travis*, tends to forget this. Transactional Travis sees networking as a series of quid pro quos—he's willing to scratch your back but only if he knows you're going to scratch his. For that reason, you may be hesitant to even seek help from him because you know there will be strings attached and it may end up costing you more down the line.

Transactional Travis treats relationships the way a bad farmer might treat their crops. If a crop takes six months to grow, you'd be a bad farmer to try to reap the harvest just six *weeks* after you've sown the seeds. You haven't let the seeds you've sown fully develop into something you can benefit from. Investments of relationship capital work the same way—you have to give them time to appreciate.

Avoid being Transactional Travis by remembering the lessons from the previous chapter about sowing now and reaping later—the spiritual lesson of karma, or the business project of superpower R&D. Transactional Travis may be frustrated by networking that doesn't seem to be paying off quickly enough, but approaching connection this way will not lead to the deep, meaningful, long-term, and really valuable type of relationships we need to pursue our treasure.

Making Meaningful Connections

These characters—Surface-Level Sarah, Oscar the Opportunist, and Transactional Travis—teach us lessons about how *not* to approach networking. But they also remind us of one of the core lessons of the connection journey: meaningful relationships are something you invest in by giving, and the benefit you will receive comes later and sometimes in unexpected ways. This gives us our first lesson in how you *should* approach networking: remember that relationships are a two-way street and that, if you want something from someone, often the best way to get it is by asking how *you* can help *them*. This demonstrates that you have something to offer, ideally our superpower and cultural value, such that you will, in turn, be worth investing in for them.

OK, I can hear you saying, *I get that, but that's still kind of abstract. I want to know how to be a better networker, which means knowing things like who I should connect with and what to say to them!*

Of course, there are whole books on networking, but I can give you the outlines of what I talk through with my students and mentees. Let's start with the people you need to be reaching out to. Once you've identified what your treasure is, try first to identify people who you think have attained that same treasure—who have achieved the kind of impact you want to have or are who occupy the same position you hope to attain. Who are *the* key players in the area you're interested in? Ultimately, you want to be thinking about how you get on their radar or in the same room (literally or figuratively) with them. Once you're on that radar or in that room, you can start putting your superpower on display to demonstrate that you might be a person worth investing in.

Now, these may be very accomplished people, and it may be hard to imagine being in direct contact with them. It is understandable to feel intimidated—but don't worry, you're not going to be cold-calling these people. You're going to start small, within your second ring, your existing network, and slowly connect the dots between where you are and where they are (in other words, where you want to be).

You can start connecting the dots by identifying a second group of people: those who are on the same critical path to attaining your treasure but have progressed further than you have along that path. These will also be important players in your area of interest though perhaps earlier in their careers or working at a smaller scale. Once you've identified these people, you can start to make a strategic plan to connect with them, move yourself further along your own critical path, and put yourself in closer proximity to that first group of people.

If you're still struggling to get started connecting those dots, reach out to your existing network, no matter what it is—an alumni network, a neighborhood association, a church community, whatever. Remember, the answer is in your network: even if you don't directly know someone who knows the person you're looking to connect with, you know someone who can help you progress to some degree on your critical path or accelerate past whatever obstacle is currently standing in your way. If you keep investing in these second-ring relationships and giving from your superpower, you will continually be bringing new people into your second ring, and at some point you will be connected with someone who is one degree of separation from someone you are aiming to connect with—whether that's one of the really big players or just someone who is further along on your same critical path.

When you get to that point, you can ask your immediate connection to introduce you to that person, or you can reach out to them directly. That immediate connection still helps out with your pitch when you reach out directly, because you turn what would otherwise be a cold call into a slightly warmed-up call. Any other points of connection you can draw on will warm that call up even more—do a little research on these people on LinkedIn, and find out if you are from the same state, or you're fans of the same sports team, or you went to the same school.

Of course, assuming the person you're hoping to connect with is, in fact, somewhere further along your critical path to your treasure, you also have the way paved for you a bit by the fact that you share something even more important, such as a passion, mission, or purpose, with this person. Remember, you're trying to network and make connections *with a purpose*. And that purpose is not, at the outset, asking the person if they can help you or invest in you. It's sharing with them your superpower and cultural value and telling them you're available to help them on *their* journey. If you put yourself out there as someone who is willing to invest in others, then others will see you as someone worth investing in, in turn. It also helps to keep in mind that other people love showing off *their* superpowers and passions, so when you reach out, you're giving them an opportunity to do so, which can be rewarding for them in itself.

So, we've gone full circle from *who* you need to be connecting with to *what* you need to say to them when you reach out. Share your story. Offer help. The more progress you have made on your leadership journey, working through the first three of the 5 Cs, the more confidence you will have and the more effective you will be in making connections with the people on your critical path.

This is the point Benedita had reached by the time she started accelerating on the connection portion of her own journey. Telling her story to her section and to the social enterprise club informed people immediately around her of her passion and her treasure of having positive social impact in her hometown. She then offered her puzzle-solving superpower as a resource and, as an organizer of the social enterprise club's conference, began to make more connections in the world of social entrepreneurship.

She was excited to tell me, for instance, that she had met and had lunch with a man named Xavier, an entrepreneur who had started a company to sell an educational software platform he had developed with a partner. The reason Xavier was at this conference was to speak about his efforts to develop a social-impact wing of the company focusing on connecting underprivileged school-aged children in developing countries with the software he had developed.

He had piloted programs in Nigeria and Kenya, so his focus was currently in Africa, but his mission spoke directly to what Benedita wanted to do back in São Paulo. He shared insights with her on the hands-on aspects of running a social enterprise, and she offered advice based on the operational acumen she had developed at BCG and the finance knowledge she had developed at HBS—even suggesting creative solutions to a few operational puzzles for him. In doing so, she displayed her superpower, showed her willingness to invest in Xavier, and demonstrated that she could be worth investing in as well—in other words, establishing the kind of meaningful connection that would move her forward on her leadership journey.

Relationship Capital Returns

Toward the end of June that year, I joined Benedita on a video call to check in with her on how her summer was going.

"I'm winding down my six weeks with BCG," she told me, "and then I'll have the next six weeks to do something else. I honestly thought that the BCG part might be kind of a drag, because I wasn't sure I was feeling it. It's good to be able to save some money, but I can't get excited about helping the local oil and gas firm with their operational challenges. However, in addition to being *thrilled* to be able to be back in my hometown and spend time with family, I've had a really great manager who's been really supportive of my social entrepreneurship aspirations. In fact, through him I've made even more connections and gotten some valuable experience."

Benedita had had to explain to her employers why she wanted to split her summer, so by the time she got to São Paulo to work, her manager was well aware of her story and her envisioned treasure. This manager himself was the chairperson of the board of a local private school that was in the process of writing its five-year strategic plan. In addition to her traditional operations work at BCG, he asked

Benedita if she might help him on some committee work he needed to do as part of that process, which gained her more experience in the educational sector and connected her to some other folks in the local philanthropy world.

"That's terrific!" I said. "You can really see how sharing your journey and your ambitions led to new connections and opportunities, even from this unexpected source. Where does that leave you for the rest of the summer, though? Do you have anything lined up?"

"As a matter of fact, I do," she said, with more confidence than I think I had ever seen in her before. "Remember Xavier?" I did. "Well, we've stayed in touch, and I've been telling him about some of the philanthropy and education connections I've made here. He's now interested in trying to adapt the programs he's developed in Nigeria and Kenya to a Latin American context, so he asked me to consult with him on education in Brazil. I told him I'd help any way I could, and I pointed out that he'd need local connections, so … well, long story short, he wants to do a pilot project in São Paulo, and he's asked me to be the local point person on operations and financing."

"That's going to be incredible hands-on experience at the grassroots level," I said.

"Exactly—just what I need to really start getting a sort of well-rounded picture of what all goes into doing what I want to do. Plus, what I really wanted to do, my treasure, was to have some impact on kids' educational prospects here, and now here I am actually starting to do it!" Her excitement came through clearly on the video call. "It's a small organization, so it doesn't pay much or, like, at all. But, hey, that's why I focused on BCG work for the first part of summer!"

Apart from a small stipend, Benedita would essentially be working as a volunteer, but she appreciated the fact that this was an opportunity for her to sow seeds that would bear fruit down the line.

If nothing else, the opportunity to do work that she was passionate about and to gain experience she would certainly benefit from made the enterprise worth it. She was learning a great deal and developing the skills she would need surrounding her superpower to really pursue her treasure. She had learned some of the high-level administrative and finance side of things at HBS and in her work with her manager at BCG, but now she would really be participating in the entrepreneurial journey of trying to build something from the ground up, to scale it, and to convince investors to fund it. She was getting the view from the bottom up in addition to the top down, so to speak.

Benedita was making key connections with several people who would play a role on the critical path to her treasure: accomplished executives in nonprofit leadership positions in her hometown, leaders in education, social entrepreneurs who were a little further on the critical path than she was, and impact investors who would help fund the project she was helping with. She learned that summer that she had the skills to operate on the same level as those people and to bring value to what they were working on—she belonged in the room with them and was well on her way to cultivating the network of social sector leaders that she would be able to leverage to attain her treasure. The network started to grow organically as she invested her experience and relationship capital—and above all, her leadership capital—in others.

TERRI BRADLEY ON THE BENEFIT OF ADVISORS

Terri talks about the importance of relationships, especially with advisors, to building Brown Toy Box:

> I think part of being able to get things happening in the business has been my ability to build relationships and building relation-

ships long before I even needed them or knew why … Most of my advisors I met on LinkedIn. And that was just me reaching out, being very authentic: "Hey, this is what I'm building, here are my gaps, here's where I see you're very strong, and can we talk about how we're going to disrupt generational poverty for Black kids?" And most of the people that I reached out to being very authentic in that way … enjoy pouring into someone that they think is going to do something [with their advice].

You have to have your tribe, your advisors, and your mentors. And I think you have to be conscious and be considerate of each of those groups' time. You've got to be considerate of what they pour into you, and implement it, and then say, "This is what I've done."

Your Personal Board of Advisors

On that same video call, I encouraged Benedita to start thinking about another key component of her network: that close-in group of people that would make up her personal board of advisors. I encourage students and mentees to think about making up a personal board by drawing from three general categories of people.

The first are the ones I'll call the *hall-of-famers*. At some point on your connection journey, you'll connect with one of the big players in whatever arena your treasure lies in—someone who has achieved something close to your own personal BHAG. This person is a hundred miles ahead of you on the critical path, so there's no competition between the two of you. They may be starting to think about the legacy portion of their treasure—having more third-ring impact by influencing the next generation of leaders—so they're happy to share some lessons and insight with someone coming up behind them who may have been in their third ring but who has a compelling pitch and seems worth investing in.

For me personally as a teacher and coach, the exemplar here is Dr. James "Jim" Cash. Jim is a legend at HBS. He was teaching there when I was a student, and his name is now on one of the buildings there. He cares deeply about the school, about educating business leaders, and about the representation of Black professors on campus. He's a *thousand* miles ahead of me in terms of impact, but I'm lucky enough to have access to him where I can call him to ask questions about a range of subjects, from teaching to board governance. People like this can give you an objective overview and helpful advice about navigating the critical path to whatever your treasure is.

The second category of people is what I'll call the *rising stars*. These are folks who are ahead of you on the critical path but maybe 10 miles ahead instead of a hundred (or a thousand). They're still on their way to their treasure and are much closer to where you currently are in your journey. They can give more concrete advice about what you need to do to keep moving forward. They can speak directly to some of the challenges you're facing here and now, because they faced them not too long ago.

Benedita had found a potential rising-star advisor in Xavier. He was just a little older than she was and still getting started on his social enterprise, but he was further along than she was and could reach back and give her a hand in a way. In my case, I can seek specific advice from a handful of the professors I work with who have been around for a decade or so longer than I have. They know the challenges we're facing directly, but we're not competing with each other, so they can serve as advisors to me.

Finally, you have your *pit crew*. These are folks who are close to you personally—maybe family, maybe friends—who may have no expertise whatsoever on the type of career or goal that you're pursuing but who know *you* and who you're comfortable enough with to be open with them. There's nothing professional at stake in your relationship, but you can draw on their knowledge of you and your values to help you align what you may be trying to do professionally with who you really are as a person. When you need to pull off the racetrack for some maintenance, so to speak, your pit crew is there waiting for you.

Unlike a corporate or nonprofit board of advisors, these three categories of people never need to be in the same room with one another to hash things out. You can seek them out in different areas and for different purposes and try to triangulate the different types of advice you get to develop an insight on how to move forward.

Having someone on your personal board involves taking a connection you've made in your network to the next level, so to speak. You need to know that you can trust them and be safe with them. In each case, these need to be people who you can be open and honest with, and they'll be open and honest with you, in turn. They'll also serve the function of holding you accountable to what you say you're going to do or what you need to do. You've personally connected with them, and now they're a resource you can draw on to bounce ideas off, seek counsel from, or ask for help.

Whatever your treasure is, you can't attain it on your own. When you face obstacles, the answer is in your network. And again, that doesn't mean you have to be a rock star networker. If you invest in relationships, those investments will pay off for you. You have put yourself in a position where others are willing to invest in you and help you on your own journey.

Coaching Tips

- List five people in your third ring whom you admire and who could be located along the critical path to your treasure. Look them up on LinkedIn, and start connecting the dots between your immediate network, your second ring, and them. If you know someone who could arrange it, ask for an introduction. And when you reach out to them, tell them about your superpower and ask them how it might be useful to them. Then ask if they would be able to have an informational interview with you.

- List three organizations you'd like to be involved with to get you on the path to your treasure or that are doing exciting work that you'd like to emulate. Find out who the leaders are in those organizations, see if they are on LinkedIn, and try to connect the dots between your existing network and those people.

- I do these first two exercises with students all the time, and they're always amazed: they may not bat a thousand, but they'll get informational interviews with at least a couple of the people they reach out to. Don't be afraid of rejection.

- I'll steal this one from my friend Terri Bradley: if you are going to a networking event and you're nervous about it or unsure what to do, set yourself a very concrete goal. For instance, I'm going to stay for at least one hour, meet three new people, learn these two things about each of them, and tell them this one thing about myself. Stay until you've accomplished your goal.

- Do you have anyone on your personal board of advisors yet? Consider each of the three categories, and list one person from each who is either on your board or could be a candidate for your board. If no Hall of Famers or rising stars come to mind, return to the networking exercises I just mentioned.

- Once you've made a connection with someone, follow up and follow through. Cultivate the relationship, and you're well on your way to having a network that you can leverage on your leadership journey.

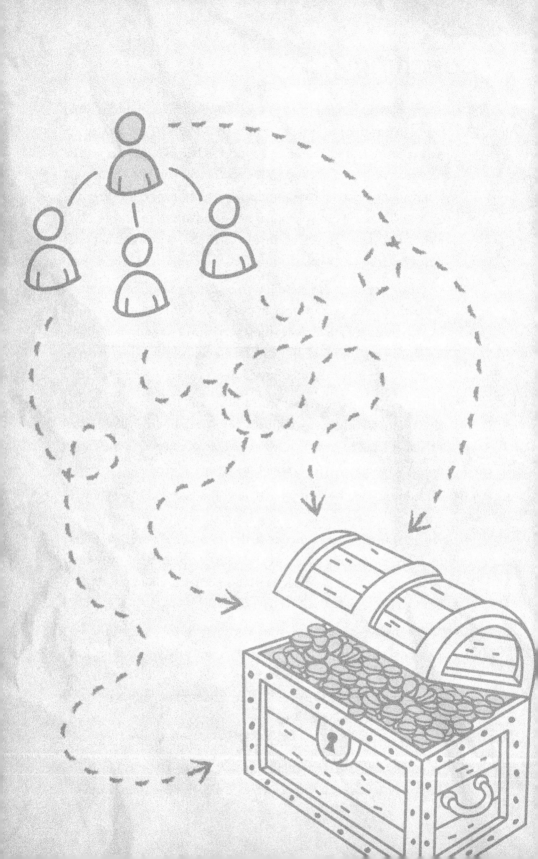

CHAPTER 10:

Confidence: My Story

*To soar toward what's possible, you must
leave behind what's comfortable.*

—*CICELY TYSON, JUST AS I AM*

Confidence is the last of the 5 Cs we'll talk about, but I'm sure you will have noticed that it has also been a thread running through the whole leadership journey. The whole project culminates in confidence, and the confidence journey is taking place at every step along the way. You build your confidence with every small achievement within the other four Cs.

It builds, first, as you start to recognize and then exercise your superpower in the capability journey. It builds further as you come to appreciate the value that your cultural background brings with it. You start telling yourself a different story about yourself, and with communication, you start sharing that story with the world. The positive feedback and results you get from that act as more confidence boosters. Finally, you gain more confidence as you start investing in relationships, helping other people on their journeys by sharing your superpower with them, and reaping the dividends from those connections—the art of giving and receiving that makes up the connection journey.

So, what's the confidence journey? As I've said from the beginning, one of the core lessons of the leadership capital framework is that *the cave you fear to enter holds the treasure you seek*. The confidence journey lies in actively exploring your cave in pursuit of your treasure.

Now, I don't mean to imply by this that there has to be *one big treasure*—the one thing you're hoping to attain—and *one big cave* that you have to conquer in order to attain it. You certainly may well have such a treasure—a BHAG—and such a cave, but along your journey to find that treasure, you will face (and have already faced) many caves containing smaller treasures. Even the other steps of the leadership journey, the other four Cs, are all like small quests into a cave (e.g., fear of rejection) in order to obtain a treasure (such as the reward of asking for the order). All these steps require confidence, and they build confidence, in turn.

Hence the importance of small wins, which work as a sort of confidence accelerator. As you accumulate them, you gain confidence, which allows you to pursue larger wins and attain greater confidence, in turn. You'll meet with failure along the way, of course. At the same time, though, you'll reach a tipping point where you start to benefit from a flywheel effect, and you can maintain forward momentum in spite of setbacks because the rewards of treasure outweigh the risks of failure (whether real or perceived). This is the point you're trying to reach in the confidence journey.

You've already made it a long way toward this goal just by working through the other four Cs. And now, if you do have that one big treasure in that one big cave, the next step of the confidence journey is simple: just go in.

Simple, but not easy, of course. But now I hope you're at a point where you recognize that the reward outweighs the perceived risk—even your worst nightmare in terms of failure or fear of rejection. I hope you're emboldened to start at least tiptoeing into that cave.

Where does my own confidence journey come into all this, though? I'll tell you about my big treasure and my big cave and about my first tiptoeing steps into that cave—one of which is the book that you're reading right now.

Stepping Out

I am generally at ease with people. I get along well with others in one-on-one situations and small groups, and I'm comfortable in front of a classroom and when I do public speaking engagements. I'm pretty good at these things, actually, and I'm comfortable because I can see the people I'm talking to. I can tailor the story I'm telling to needs of the moment. I can look out at a bunch of faces looking back at me and gauge the mood of the group. I can read the room and work an audience, telling jokes when it suits the mood or dialing the humor back for a certain audience who would find it inappropriate. If someone misunderstands or disagrees with something I say, I can engage them directly to clarify or to discuss.

All of these are a big part of my superpower as a teacher and coach. I am very effective in exercising my superpower with people I'm directly in contact with—people, basically, in my second ring. Notice, though, that this limits my impact. If I'm only communicating with people who are literally in the same room with me, then I'm not having third-ring impact, impact on the broader world at large. And I know, now, that that's where my treasure lies—in exercising my superpower to have third-ring impact.

But once my coaching gets out into the third ring, I start to feel like I have less control over it. I was nervous about writing a book, for instance, because once it's published, it's out there, open to criticism and out of my control. I can't dial back any jokes for certain readers but not others, and if someone misunderstands me, I can't step in to clarify. And honestly, that freaks me out a little bit! Opening myself up to this broader third-ring audience, whether it's through the book, through speaking and thought leadership, or through increasing work in the world of board governance, is my cave.

So, very clearly in my case, the treasure I seek—having exponentially larger impact as a coach—lies in the cave I fear to enter.

To conquer this cave and attain this treasure, I knew that I needed to break it down into a series of smaller caves, smaller treasures, that I could carefully venture into one by one in order to start accumulating some small wins that would get my confidence accelerator going. Among these caves, I knew, were the teaching cave, the book cave, and the governance cave. In each of these areas, I developed a crawl-walk-run plan to start tiptoeing into the cave. If I could work my way through these caves, I would have built a large part of the portfolio of a career coach having third-ring impact.

I could even draw on the confidence I'd built up from previous small wins in this area. As I've mentioned, my leadership journey started way back when I was an eleven-year-old quarterback for my peewee football team. Even then, though I didn't realize it at the time, I was starting to build my competence in coaching in small ways. I wouldn't have volunteered for the position of quarterback because I wasn't comfortable with it, but my coach put me in that uncomfortable position, and I just tried to make the best of it. And the series of small wins my team achieved built my confidence, in turn. So, my confidence journey began all the way back there.

We've all had these types of confidence-building experiences, and you can find some in your life story if you go looking. They may not always be positive experiences. Mine is a cute little peewee football story, but other folks have stories of surviving hard times or tough situations, and these can be drawn on to build confidence just as much as the positive stories of wins and accomplishments.

I also had to basically tiptoe into my cave, so I had to develop a crawl-walk-run plan. After all, one of the first puzzles I faced when grappling with coaching being my superpower was the practical side of it: How does a coach eat? How would I pay my bills? Clearly, at least at the beginning, I'm going to have to keep doing the things I'm already doing that I'm good at, specifically in the investing area, while I start tiptoeing into coaching. I do enjoy investing, and it provided for me. It continues to do so to some degree. M&A remains part of my portfolio career, though I have managed to shift it to being more like 20 percent of my work instead of 80 percent.

Keeping one toe in the M&A world helped alleviate some of my fears about diving into a coaching career. It's important to emphasize that confidence is not about completely overcoming or getting rid of fear but about facing fear and not allowing it to prevent your forward progress. It's about mustering the courage to tackle the unknowns and the uncomfortable parts of your journey. You may be afraid to enter the cave, but the confidence journey involves identifying what that cave is and making a plan to enter it.

GREG WALTON ON BUILDING YOUR
CONFIDENCE WITH SMALL WINS

Greg offers some insight on the work of building confidence:

> I've had so many opportunities to build my confidence. I feel
> like some of us naturally have it. I feel like in some ways I
> naturally had it, but you still have to work to build it. As early
> as middle school, I was always one to get in front of folks and
> perform at talent shows, and just be the class clown in some
> ways ... but I still had to work to build my confidence, and I
> had a lot of opportunities to do that.
>
> I was explaining this to my son last night. We were at a playoff
> game, semifinals for baseball, and he didn't pitch all year and he
> wasn't confident about it at all. He felt he was going to throw
> wild pitches all over the place. And I had to tell him, "Listen,
> I'm nervous 99 percent of the time that I'm doing speeches or
> I'm giving talks, even if I know what I'm talking about—it's
> natural. But you've got to get in the ring to help build your
> confidence that the next time you're in it, you'll be better, you'll
> feel more confident, you'll feel more natural in doing it." And
> he went up and pitched yesterday for the first time in a playoff
> game and did well. And, man, overcoming your fears in that
> sense, being able to do that, was really cool to see.

Tiptoeing In

My teaching cave centered around fear of rejection and failure. I
wanted to teach at the highest level, educating the next generation
of executives and entrepreneurs—so where better to do that than at
Harvard Business School? But I had never taught anywhere before.

What if they say no? What if I'm not cut out for it? Again, I boosted my confidence by going through the course catalog and listing all the classes I thought I could teach right away. I also made a list of all the ways I had already been interacting with students in productive and positive ways, to remind myself that I had something valuable to offer. I assured myself in this way that I was capable—I shifted the story I was telling myself, and that made me more effective when it came time to tell it to others and ask for the order of getting a teaching position.

Doing this work was the tiptoeing, the crawling part of my crawl-walk-run plan. It got me to a point where I felt comfortable enough to walk—to actually ask for the job. It was also important to remind myself at this point what the risk was if I met with failure. What would happen in the worst-case scenario? I would be told no, and I'd have to go to plan B. That's it. Realizing that failure is rarely fatal—even the worst-case scenario is not that serious—is another good way to boost your confidence.

Similarly, for my governance journey, I had already been serving as a director on the boards of some nonprofit organizations and in connection with some of my private equity work. In this case, I knew I had the basic skill set. Still, though, in the early part of my governance journey, if I was on a board of directors, I was there as a representative of a private equity fund. That's what gave me the credibility to get on those boards. I used to joke that I bought my way onto the board with someone else's money. Behind this joke was a real insecurity about what I really brought to the table in those situations. Most of the other guys (and yes, they were mostly guys) in the room were C-suite from other major companies, and most of them didn't look like me. My treasure was to add real value at that level, but my cave was the fear of not belonging—not being old enough, connected enough, or experienced enough.

I tiptoed in by gathering some credentials, getting some formal training through the National Association of Corporate Directors on the role of a director and the full scale of a director's duties and responsibilities. This helped me realize, to go back to the first two Cs, that this work would in fact be leveraging my superpower and that I had something unique to offer organizations based on my cultural balance sheet. Once I embraced my coaching superpower, the board and governance opportunities started opening up. I started focusing on adding value as a teacher and coach—a nontraditional path for a board member—and that's how I articulated the unique value that I would bring to the table. That added value is more important than any title I might have. And that's how I've attained my treasure in this area—adding value to companies that are having impact at a global level.

So, I had to tiptoe into this position too and build up small wins by showing that I added value on the boards of much smaller and more local organizations. This built up my confidence so that I could tell myself and others the story of how I belonged in that room, even if I don't look like everyone else and didn't get into that room through the same path.

The folks who presented me with opportunities, both in teaching and in governance, ultimately saw the value I offered too and realized that I could benefit the students and the organizations I would be working with. I could chronicle both these journeys across the other four Cs—and I have done so, to some extent, with my teaching journey—but the core of what I was doing there was building confidence through small wins in order to tiptoe into my caves and move toward my treasure.

My teaching and governance journeys have led to increasingly big wins that have further built the confidence I need to leverage my impact from my second ring to my third ring. One of the first ways

I did this was through this book, which itself involved a tiptoeing process—reaching out feelers to publishers, consulting experts, and seeking advice from folks in my network who had also written and published books. I'm also branching out into other media, such as podcasting.

I'm past the practical fears at this point and in the realm of ego and pride. What happens if no one loves the book? What if no one listens to the podcast? Here is where the flywheel of the confidence accelerator kicks in. The potential rewards of attaining my treasure, which I've gotten a taste of with the impact I've had so far, are so great that they totally outweigh the risk involved. I can see from the large but still limited number of people I have successfully coached that I could potentially have that impact on an indefinite number of people who may never sit in my classroom or meet me face-to-face. For even one person outside of my network, my second ring, to find value in what I'm saying, to have their life changed in some way so that they can follow their passion, find their superpower, or progress further on their leadership journey—the potential reward of that far outweighs the fear. My ego and pride concerns seem insignificant compared to that.

When you reach that level where the rewards of pursuing your treasure outweigh the fears and the risks involved, then you've hit that confidence accelerator level where you're able to push on in spite of adversity, and you're so empowered that you can keep pursuing your treasure even when your confidence takes a hit. In the next chapter, we'll dig deeper on how to identify and explore those caves so that you can start tiptoeing into them and ultimately making strides toward attaining your treasure.

TERRI BRADLEY ON HER CAVE

Terri reports that one of the caves she fears, one of the biggest risks she worries about, concerns the unique challenges of being a Black woman entrepreneur:

> The cave is feeling exposed sometimes. And it's not even about ego. Feeling exposed is not about, "Oh, I'm personally going to be embarrassed." It's such a crappy place for Black entrepreneurs because I feel like I'm carrying everybody on my back. The whole world is watching, and if I fuck it up, then I fuck it up for everybody … And it's not just my imagination. I know if I don't perform well in Target, the next [Black entrepreneur] that comes along that says, "I'm an educational toy company, and we're trying to disrupt generational poverty," [the big companies] will be like, "Yeah, we heard that spiel before."
>
> So that is what keeps me up at night. How do I perform? How do I do these things? How do I make sure that as I kick open a door, I make sure that it stays open and it's wide enough and I'm making it where more people can have a seat at the table? So I feel this pressure that I bring my people in, and I'm carrying them into every room with me.

Prompts for Reflection

- After working through the other four Cs, what obstacles remain to you pursuing your treasure? This may be where your cave lies.

- What small wins have you achieved in your journey so far that can help get your confidence accelerator going?

CHAPTER 11:

Confidence: Your Story

Most people run from what they're afraid of. I run toward it. That doesn't mean I think I'm bulletproof (I've learned the hard way that I'm not) or that I'm unaware of danger. I experience fear as much as the next man. But one of the greatest mistakes people can make is becoming comfortable with their fears.

—CURTIS "50 CENT" JACKSON, HUSTLE HARDER, HUSTLE SMARTER

Benedita returned to HBS for her second year energized from her summer experiences. She had made a lot of connections and gained considerable experience in running an educational social impact project, both from a strategic and operational perspective and from the fundraising perspective. She had also done some analysis of the impact investing world as part of helping her manager with the strategic plan for the school whose board he chaired, so she was starting to learn about the finance side of the nonprofit and social enterprise world.

She was really starting to feel the magic of putting her superpower of creative puzzle-solving into operation in these different contexts, and she was having impact in her hometown in the area of education, which meant her treasure was within reach like it had never been before. The two projects she had worked on introduced her to two very different types of networks, each of which could open the door to mutually beneficial relationships. The first included established and successful individuals and organizations that could provide her with mentorship, and the second included younger leaders, such as Xavier, who were just a little further down the path than she was and who she could see herself in.

"Working on Xavier's project was like touching my dream project more closely than I ever have before," she told me during our first meeting since her return. She had just gotten back to Boston and was gearing up for the semester, registering for classes, and figuring out what else she might want to do for the next year. "It's just getting off the ground, but it's something that could really have an impact on kids in my community. And working with Xavier—and watching him work with the handful of other people involved—was kind of like seeing where I might be myself a few years down the line."

I asked her what she was thinking of doing moving forward.

"Well, I don't really know. BCG is wanting me to come back, but I also have a tentative offer of a job with Xavier—if he's able to get all the funding he needs for the Brazil project. There's also a woman I met through my work on that school's board who runs a social impact investment firm. She told me to look her up after I graduated, as she might be able to find me a position there."

"Sounds like you're racking up some wins! How does that make you feel?"

"It's exciting!" she said. "There's just one aspect I'm still nervous about. A lot of things keep circling back to finance and this whole world of impact investing, and you know that investment/finance stuff still intimidates me."

"Well, you're coming at it from a position of strength," I said. "You've been learning about the field, not to mention talking to folks in impact investing, and it sounds like you've had some success. You also have another year of coursework to keep working on your capability in that area."

"That's true. This woman in Brazil looked at my pitch document for Xavier's project and said it was really strong, and she also showed me some of the portfolio of projects her firm has invested in there in São Paulo. It's really exciting stuff."

"Well, are you going to take my Investing for Impact course?"

She laughed. "Yay, more finance coursework."

I smiled. "Well, that's the thing about impact investing: you've got to have the investing in there if you want to have the impact. I also know some folks at a Boston-based impact fund who could probably use some part-time help. They even have some education projects in their portfolio. That might be a way to start tiptoeing into that world a little more."

Her eyes widened, and she took a deep breath. "OK—I think I might be able to do that."

Benedita was coming face-to-face with a core lesson of the leadership capital framework: *The cave you fear to enter holds the treasure you seek.* Her cave, the world of high finance, lay on her route to achieving the type of impact she wanted to have. Even if she did not pursue impact investment itself as a career, she would at least need to be able to speak the language of those people in order to make a business case and raise funding for whatever enterprise she ended up pursuing.

Her anxiety about her capability in the realm of finance was what had brought her into my office in the first place almost a year before.

She hadn't spent time on Wall Street (as some of her classmates had) or followed the traditional path of the money manager. She knew, however, that she was going to have to stretch and get out of her comfort zone a little bit in order to make progress on what she really wanted to do. A job with a local impact investing firm would be a low-stakes way to start tiptoeing into that.

All along the way, Benedita could have played it much safer than she did. She had already achieved success and status with her position at BCG, and continuing in that position without branching out would have carried much more security and much less risk along with it. Stepping away from that safety—letting go of the side of the pool, as I like to put it—was already tackling a huge cave for her. She could have stayed close to the side of the pool in order to avoid the risk of failure.

But staying put came at an even greater cost: denying her passion and not leveraging her superpower to pursue her treasure. Avoiding the risk of failure also means giving up on the potential rewards of success, just as staying at the side of the pool deprives you of the joy of swimming. And, as we saw with her experience over the summer, letting go of the side of the pool had allowed her to rack up several small wins that started building her confidence—getting the flywheel of her confidence accelerator going. This set her up for what may be the most challenging part of the overall leadership journey: the confidence journey, in which she had to find hidden courage within herself to venture into the cave that she knew held her treasure.

As with Benedita, pursuing your treasure and entering your cave is most likely not going to be a "one and done" experience. You will go through a journey of discovering small caves, and in each case, you have to decide whether you enter and search for your treasure, or whether you stay outside in the safety of the status quo. As you discover small treasures and make small wins along your journey, you will build your confidence more and more to keep searching and exploring new and bigger caves and attaining new and bigger treasures. To attain those treasures, though, you have to put something on the line and enter the caves in the first place.

This means risk, and risk means fear. Fear requires confidence—and you can build confidence by developing a crawl-walk-run plan, just as I had to do when I embarked on my coaching journey. But what does a plan like this really look like? Let's take it step-by-step.

TERRI BRADLEY ON HER TREASURE

Terri is frank about her treasure:

> Well, there are two answers to *What is my treasure?* There's an impact answer, and there's a business answer.
>
> The impact answer is changing the trajectory of all of these Black children's lives that have been locked out. Full stop.
>
> The business answer is, I want to be a player. I want to be at the table with the Melissa and Dougs. I remember a few years ago I was at Invest Atlanta, and we were presenting to their board … and I said, "I'm going to be the largest toy company"—I didn't say "Black owned"—I said "*the* largest toy company out of the southeast. So what Home Depot has done, what Coca-Cola has done, I want y'all to talk about Brown Toy Box in that same way." And I still mean that.

Starting to Crawl

The first step, the *crawl*, involves work mostly done on your own, reflecting on your situation—much as the leadership journey started with self-reflection in getting to know your superpower and your culture, the confidence journey starts with getting to know your treasure and your cave.

Start, then, with a *treasure analysis*. What treasure do you really seek? What does it really look like in action in your own life? How does it inform and shape your day-to-day life? Does it pay the bills, or will you have to do that some other way? Is there a job title attached to it, or are you going to have to build some new portfolio-type career?

Go back to my description of discovering my coaching and teaching superpower, and you'll discover that this is exactly what I was doing. *How does a coach pay the bills? What should I put on my résumé?* Even before I started putting my new story about myself as a coach out in the world, I was asking myself these questions.

The treasure analysis is also closely linked to your understanding of your relationships to the three rings that make up our social relationships. What do you want to accomplish in each of those three rings? For the first ring, just yourself, what kind of work will you have to do to develop yourself in the direction of your treasure? Some of the practicalities you need to tackle to move forward will fall into this category—perhaps you need to finish some schooling or credentialing, or you have some debt you need to get off the books so you can more productively invest your money moving forward. You may also have treasures that lie in this ring—a certain level of athletic accomplishment, for instance, or developing your patience and emotional resilience.

Most of us, however, seek treasures that lie outside the first ring, that touch people in either the second or the third rings. What treasures do you seek at the level of your family and immediate community? You may wish to start a family or to better support or engage with the family you already have. You may also want to contribute to your community or support your friends in a certain way. There is really no limit to the types of treasures people might locate at this level.

For many people, contributing to and benefiting from their immediate community may be where their big treasure lies, and this is great. If you are one of these people, you still have important caves to conquer and important contributions to make—you're still on a confidence and leadership journey. If you hope to have third-ring impact, however, your treasure and your cave will be different still.

In any case, your treasure analysis lies simply in determining what you really desire or wish for—your BHAG—at each of these levels, within each of these rings. The next question is what is getting in the way of you accomplishing these goals or attaining these treasures. This is your *cave analysis*.

Is there something you know you need to do to move forward in accomplishing your goals, but for some reason you just can't bring yourself to do it? If you know where you want to go—what your treasure is—but are having trouble moving in that direction, you need to identify what the obstacles to your progress really are. If you can focus on the reasons for your lack of progress, you can most likely start to identify your cave somewhere within those reasons.

Even identifying your cave, speaking its name out loud, can be scary, but it can also be a breakthrough. This is because fear is often overstated or irrational, and by identifying and describing our cave, we start to apply some rational thought to it that moves us in the direction of making it less scary. Let's be literal about it for a minute: Why would you be afraid to go into a cave, especially if you knew there was a treasure in there? *It's dark in there!* Well, fear of the dark is not necessarily rational. *Well, in this case it is, because if I can't see, I could fall and get hurt, or there might be something hiding in there.* OK, so we can start thinking rationally about the risks. What sorts of things are you afraid of? *Bears. And snakes.* Again, we're applying rational thought here: Are there bears in this area? Are the snakes around here dangerous? What's the risk, *really*?

You get the idea. Similarly, with the metaphorical cave that contains your treasure, you can start applying some critical analysis to it and realize that some of what makes you fearful isn't really rational. A clearheaded approach to the risks involved in entering your cave will remind you of a lesson I've mentioned several times before: *failure is rarely fatal.* What will the real challenges be, and what will really be at risk if you tempt failure?

Overall, the challenges that you really face in entering your cave fall broadly into two buckets. First, there are the practicalities: Do you have enough money and resources to set out in pursuit of whatever your goal is? Do you have the right contacts in your network? It's easy to convince yourself that you're lacking something or that, whatever your goal is, you'll have to pursue it later because you just *can't right now.*

And you may not be wrong! I certainly faced this when I started my coaching journey. But you can still take the first step—even if you're still just crawling!—which is to clearly outline to yourself exactly what those challenges are, what you *do* need that you don't currently have, and start making a plan to attain those things and overcome these obstacles step-by-step. This is why I have pursued coaching and teaching while keeping one foot in the investment world.

The second challenge bucket concerns your ego. What are the risks to your pride of setting off in pursuit of this new goal? What are the risks to your ego if you stumble along the way? Again, I had to tackle this at the beginning of my coaching journey. *I'm a successful investment professional, and now I'm going to show up calling myself a coach? How is that going to sound at the next cocktail party? What if no one buys it? What if I write my book and the messages don't resonate?*

But again, what do you really risk? What is the likelihood of the worst-case scenario coming to pass? And how bad is that scenario *really*? If you hold fast to your values and your integrity, you can recover from failure.

You'll also often discover that there is not just one big, monolithic cave standing there facing you but rather a series of smaller caves that you can tackle step-by-step. There may be some low-hanging fruit, some small caves that you can conquer easily and start to rack up some small wins so that you start getting your confidence accelerator going. Once we're doing that, though, we've moved to the *walking* part of the crawl-walk-run plan. You've laid out a game plan, and now you're going to put it into action, even if it's just a little bit at a time. When you start walking into your cave, it's OK, and often even prudent, to tiptoe a little bit.

GREG WALTON ON HIS OWN TREASURE ANALYSIS

In our interview, Greg reflected on what his own treasure analysis might look like at this juncture in his life:

> I can't eliminate the parental aspect, because I feel like once you have kids and you're in the throes of raising them, most of your effort is centered around just trying to create good human beings ... because they're going to impact hundreds and thousands more people throughout their journey. And if we're doing the best job that we can to try to raise them, that's going to go farther than anything I could do, because hopefully they've got a longer run than me. So that's number one.

Number two would be taking that next step on the journey of thinking beyond just the organizations that I've been connected to … I've got to get more connected beyond Year Up in a sense and be more *Greg, the entity*, and not *Greg, the vice chairman of Year Up and alum of Year Up*, to where I'm really starting to get in other spaces … I know I'm going to be a beacon of the Second Chance Act, that we are greater than our mistakes, and I'm really starting to [be a champion for] formerly incarcerated folks and people who were in the foster care system and age out, who can't get access to resources to try to navigate being an adult.

I need to take the opportunity to think: What am I doing? Why am I here? What's my full purpose? What are some of the things I can tap into? And I know more often than not, it's making a positive impact in people's lives. So not one treasure, a lot of different things.

Walking Carefully

The walk portion of the crawl-walk-run plan involves, most generally speaking, taking some personal strides, on your own, toward entering your cave. This is not about conquering the cave on your own but about starting to take experimental steps. To go back to our literal cave for a moment: if you're worrying about stumbling and falling in the dark, what happens if you grab a flashlight and a walking stick? Does that help make the challenge more manageable? Most important, does it allow you to take some first, tentative steps into your cave?

So the walking phase can be tentative and experimental, testing your fears against actual attempts to overcome them. This is where your small wins come in: as you take early steps and tackle some of the easier mini-caves, your confidence starts to build, and your fear of the other caves or the big cave starts to shrink. Once you're in there, you may find out that the cave isn't so scary after all.

I've mentioned that writing this book was a cave for me. For me, the walk phase involved some information gathering on writing a book by talking to publishers and other folks who had written books. It also involved some smaller, lower-stakes forays into writing, such as posting some articles on LinkedIn, as well as giving talks on the 5 Cs in a lot of different contexts so that I could build my confidence that my messages did resonate with a wide range of people.

I teach and coach a lot of ambitious young people, and this strategy of starting with small wins is one that I share with all of them. As accomplished as students already have to be to get into HBS, you'd still be amazed at how the confidence portion of the journey is the hardest for most of them. Like most of us, they still have a confidence deficit. We saw this with Benedita, but she is not unique in this respect.

In teaching entrepreneurship, a lot of what I'm trying to impart is a willingness to experiment, a process for effective experimentation, and an understanding that it's all right to try something and fail. Even trying is accomplishing *something*. If you want to pursue something entrepreneurial, but you're in a job at a larger organization and you don't feel up to the risk of leaving it, try something *intra*preneurial. Offer to lead some internal initiative. The less confident and more afraid you feel, the smaller the initiative can be. Maybe it's just a weekend charity drive. Even if it's not in your main area of interest or expertise, this at least starts to get you in the habit of taking some chances and experimenting. Better yet, if it goes well, you've got a win that can get your confidence accelerator going so you can move on to the next thing.

In whatever situation you find yourself now, even if you're in a large organization that you can't afford to turn your back for practical reasons, you can start to take some chances, try some experimentation, and take some entrepreneurial risks that will move you forward in your journey and help you start to develop your leadership capital.

Benedita took the tentative step of offering part-time help at the Boston-based impact fund I connected her with. She offered up her puzzle-solving superpower, and they were happy to have her perspective. She went quickly from feeling like a total finance novice to feeling confident in her ability to figure things out and make her way in that world.

"I'm actually helping with the funding for some educational initiatives, and I'm really able to contribute even though I'm no finance guru," she told me in a meeting a couple of months into the semester. "And I'm really amazed at how much ... well, impact you can have with an impact fund. Which gave me an idea ..."

Benedita went on to pitch me on the idea of doing an independent project with her in which she would write the business plan for her own São Paulo–based educational impact fund. I agreed, and the two of us spent the rest of the semester working on how she might go about raising money and structuring a fund for educational initiatives in her community. We worked through what an organization like that should look like, what competences and capabilities she would need to lead it, what kind of team she would need to surround herself with to augment her own capabilities, how much money she'd need to get some pilot projects off the ground, and who she would need in her network to accomplish these things.

By developing this business plan, Benedita was moving further forward on the walking phase of her own crawl-walk-run plan— experimenting, taking tentative steps, sorting out how daunting her big cave was really going to be. In fact, by enlisting my help and by drawing on the experience and expertise of other folks she had managed to draw into her network, she was taking some of the final steps of the walking portion of her journey and setting herself up to run.

Ready to Run

I'm writing this at the close of that semester of independent work with Benedita, so she has not yet put the plan into action, and in fact, I don't know when or if she will pursue exactly that plan in exactly that form.

What I do know is that she is now in running position. The running portion of your crawl-walk-run plan comes into play when you start to leverage your network and deploy the leadership capital you've accumulated to get others on board with helping you conquer your cave and attain your treasure. You may recall from the first chapter that leadership just means a social power to enlist the help of others to accomplish your goal, and once you're at the running phase of the confidence journey, then you're also at the culmination of your leadership journey.

That's not to say that your leadership journey comes to an end. As I've mentioned, there are several treasures and several caves along the way, and to succeed in conquering those caves and attaining those treasures, you'll need to leverage the leadership capital you've built through experience and relationships across your journey so far. Even if you enter the big cave and attain your main treasure—your BHAG, in whatever area of your life and whatever form it takes—there will still be new goals, new treasures, and new caves.

The rest of Benedita's story is still to be written, but it is loaded with opportunities. She is ready to start to leverage her network to attain her treasure in whatever she determines is best. She has the security of continuing at BCG for as long as she needs if she is not quite ready to make the jump into something new. If she does change, she may go the corporate route with a position at an established impact investment firm, whether that be the one in São Paulo or the one she has already been successfully helping out at in Boston. This will offer her the opportunity to continue to learn, gain experience, and develop relationships.

Or she could really dive in the deep end and strike out on her own enterprise, whether that be an education start-up, partnering with Xavier, or working to establish her own impact fund as she and I had discussed and outlined. There is more risk here, but with her network and experience, she is set up for success, or at least set up so that failure would not be fatal for her. There will be challenges—I can't promise her a fairy-tale ending. But her journey through the 5 Cs has left her, on balance, with more possibility than difficulty. The confidence journey culminates in her recognition and pursuit of those opportunities, in spite of the challenges.

Benedita's journey is not atypical. Sure, she had the advantage of being a student at HBS, which brings access to a network of professors and alumni. She had direct access to me as a coach. But, in its core elements, her journey was a journey that anyone can go on. We've heard from Greg Walton and Terri Bradley throughout this book, and each of them went on this journey without the exact same benefits and circumstances as Benedita. They all came from very different backgrounds and had very different experiences, as well as different aspirations—different treasures and different caves—but each has benefited and continues to benefit from the lessons of the 5 Cs. Their examples show that the leadership journey is accessible to anyone and can take different forms, whether that be entrepreneurial (as in Terri's case), working in the context of other organizations (as in Greg's), or taking whatever shape Benedita's journey ends up taking.

If your leadership journey has followed Benedita's journey through the first four of the 5 Cs, then you will already be well set up and equipped for the full cave exploration that makes up the running part of the confidence journey. Perhaps you've already got some small wins that have your confidence accelerator going, and you're ready to start putting your superpower, your cultural background, and your network to work on venturing into bigger caves and finding bigger treasures.

As for Benedita having the benefit of having me as a coach, well, now you have that benefit, too. The basic elements of my coaching are distilled in this book, and my hope is that you will take what I've written here and use it to help guide you in your own leadership journey. You don't have to come to Harvard and have me as a professor to benefit from what I'm trying to teach. You now have the tools to start down the path of your leadership journey on your own (and at a much lower price tag, by the way).

Everyone has goals. Everyone has experiences. Everyone has relationships. Everyone has the ability to leverage those experiences and relationships to work in tandem with other folks to achieve their goals. In other words, everyone has a hidden leader within. My goal with this book has been to help you uncover your own leader within so that in the end, you can confidently go exploring, work your way up to entering your cave, and go and find your treasure.

Coaching Tips

- If you're feeling stuck in your leadership journey, develop a crawl-walk-run plan to start making some progress.

- To crawl, first do a frank treasure analysis. Ask yourself the questions I mentioned in the chapter: What treasure do you really seek? What does it really look like in action in your own life? How does it inform and shape your day-to-day life? Does it pay the bills, or will you have to do that some other way? Is there a job title attached to it, or are you going to have to build some new portfolio-type career?

- Next, do your cave analysis—what is really keeping you from making progress toward your treasure? Say it out loud, and start to rationally and critically evaluate what the risk involved really is. Have you blown the risks out of proportion? If the risks are real, how can they be mitigated or insured against?

- Now it's time to walk, even if you just tiptoe. Start to get yourself out of your comfort zone, even if it's in small ways. What's one small step you can take in the direction of your cave?

- Taking a small step can mean securing a small win that you can leverage to get your confidence accelerator going. What small wins do you already have under your belt that you can review to help boost your confidence?

- When you're ready to run, remember, the answer is in your network. Your attainment of your treasure will be the result of leveraging the leadership capital you've accumulated over the whole of your 5 Cs' journey to draw the efforts of others into your mission.

Conclusion

*An individual has not started living until he can
rise above the narrow confines of his individualistic
concerns to the broader concerns of all humanity.*

—MARTIN LUTHER KING, JR.

As I discuss in this book, many people locate their treasure in what I call *third-ring* impact—that is, impact not just beyond themselves but also beyond their immediate community and network. And I am one of those people. That's why I wrote this book, in fact, to get the framework I use in my teaching and coaching into the hands of people I may never meet face-to-face. I want to share my lessons in places I've never been with people I've never met, and I also hope to use this expanded reach to build an expanded network around the world.

So far, I've mainly had success with coaching and teaching within my second ring. As these successes have built up my confidence, though, I have become ready to leverage my superpower into my third ring, and this book is just a part of that larger project. The ultimate expression of this effort has been the founding of the NxGen COACH Network, a platform designed to put more structure around the leadership capital framework and the 5 Cs and open it up to engagement with other coaches and leaders around the world.

Much of the framework has been based on my own experience— what has worked for me and the lessons I have learned. By making it a network, I'm trying to leverage my own connections to start to draw support from other coaches and subject matter experts in other domains, to test out their coaching techniques and solutions and have them test mine. For instance, I only scratch the surface of some of the nuts and bolts of good networking here, and there are folks out there who have been working on exactly that subject for their entire careers. The NxGen COACH Network is designed to start pulling insights in from those people.

The work that other coaches and I do through the NxGen COACH Network will, in turn, be used to develop leaders around the world. In closing, I want to speak directly to both the coaches who might come into the network and the leaders, more generally, who could benefit from the lessons we offer.

To the coaches: I've shared my story, my journey, as well as the story of Benedita, which is an amalgamation of a number of HBS student stories. I've also shared insights from Greg Walton and Terri Bradley, leaders from different backgrounds and on different paths who have also taken lessons directly from my coaching. Each of these stories has lessons that other coaches can leverage for their own benefit, but if you are a coach, I hope that you will also share *your* story, as well as those of the people who have benefited from your lessons.

One of the goals of the NxGen COACH Network is to create a vehicle for coaches to share these stories with one another. Here I want to extend an offer to individual coaches to reach out and continue some of the work begun in this book through getting connected to and expanding my network.

To the leaders: first, if you're part of an organization, I want to extend the offer to reach out as well, to have a conversation about how this coaching framework can help inside your organization by driving performance and developing *intra*preneurship among your management and talent.

More importantly, though, I want to speak to the individuals who are on their own leadership journey, whether inside a larger organization, in their personal life or community, on a board of directors or advisors, or in an entrepreneurial endeavor. I love hearing from those I coach and advise, and as you work through the ideas and the exercises in this book, I want you to share the personal stories that come out of that process with me and with the network. I want to hear your version of the Benedita story and learn about how it plays out. I'd love to hear some of the small wins you've achieved along the way to where you are today. I'd love to hear how you're leveraging your superpower and your network to have impact in your second and third rings.

So, the NxGen COACH Network is not just a platform for coaches but also aims to provide a forum for the sharing of stories among the kinds of people they coach. The more voices we have contributing, the more these stories will feed future success stories and inspire other leaders and the more impact we can all have.

In other words, while this is the end of the book, this is not the end of the conversation—in fact, it's just the beginning. I hope you'll become an active participant in the work of the network by continuing the exchange of ideas and stories. I want to hear from leaders from all sectors—not just business, but politics, the social sector, community organizing, you name it.

And don't worry if you don't see yourself as the typical leader, or if you're still working on locating that leader within. I want to hear from the *atypical* leaders even more than I do the typical ones. If you see yourself in someone like Benedita or Greg, for instance, I want to hear from you. You can still have tremendous impact within your sphere of influence, and you can have further impact by sharing your stories with the broader audience that the NxGen COACH Network provides.

And that's the last message I want to share with you. Even if your treasure is limited to the impact you have within your family or immediate community, I hope you at least start to think about the impact you can have beyond yourself and even out into the third ring. That's where my treasure, passion, and purpose lie, and that's the core of what I'm trying to accomplish with the network I've established. I'm venturing into my cave to seek my treasure of expanding my impact, and I hope you will join me on that journey.

Acknowledgments

You know I believe in team—no one achieves anything of significance alone. Thank you Lord for calling me to serve through coaching and blessing me with the gifts to coach. Homage to my ancestors for the spirit of perseverance, faith, and confidence. Thank you to my entire family for pouring love into me. Thank you Mom and Dad for unconditional and unending love and support. I am carrying forward your legacy of creating opportunity through education and entrepreneurship. Tamikia, thank you for being a great sis and for my awesome nieces (Tanzanea, Kaneisha, and Sevyn).

Truman, Leland, and Armstrong, you are my treasure. I love you and am so proud of you. Thank you for being a constant source of inspiration and pride. Tiffini, thank you for being an amazing mom for our sons.

My God daughters, Leah, Makenzie, and Riley, I look forward to helping you find your treasure.

To my friends and colleagues at Harvard Business School, Six Pillars Partners, Fleetcor, NOWaccount, Kenexa, Merrill Lynch Capital Partners, Parthenon Capital, New Profit, Year Up, Project

Evident, Elev8 Foundation, Leadership Atlanta, 100 Black Men of Atlanta, and the Executive Leadership Council, you taught me how to COACH (Create Opportunity And Cultivate Humanity) by investing in me and partnering with me to invest in others.

To the team at Forbes, especially Josh Houston, thank you for helping me bring this dream to reality.

To the all the members, partners and allies of NxGen COACH Network, especially Hueman Group, Target Marketing Digital, Shiso Firm, and Mission + Cause, thank you for supporting the effort to share my gifts and message with a global audience.

I have been blessed with friends and supporters throughout my life and all have played a part of the journey that led to this book. This includes friends from hometown to Harvard, friends from pre-school to private equity, my Morehouse brothers and so many others. Thank you all for journeying with me.

To the direct contributors, Greg Walton, Terri Bradley, and Dr. Nzinga Metzger, thank you for sharing your stories and wisdom. To those whose stories I included in this book, thank you for allowing me to tell my version of our story and use it to inspire others. To all those I have coached (including my students), thank you for letting me be a part of your journey and for helping me bring Benedita to life through your curiosity, bravery, vulnerability, and confidence.

Nicole, thank you for the blessing of partnership.

Printed in the USA
CPSIA information can be obtained
at www.ICGtesting.com
JSHW020530090224
56957JS00001B/1/J